REDUCING SOCIAL TENSION AND CONFLICT

Through the Group Conversation Method

REDUCING

Foreword by IRA PROGOFF

SOCIAL TENSION
AND CONFLICT

Through the Group Conversation Method

RACHEL DAVIS DuBOIS *and* MEW-SOONG LI

ASSOCIATION PRESS • NEW YORK

Contents

5

Part III: APPLICATIONS

Foreword

THE INVITATION to write this Foreword is to me a most meaningful occasion. Over a period of many years it has deeply grieved me to observe that the authors' work was receiving but a small part of the recognition it deserves. Now, this recognition is coming. And with it the promise that the approach of Group Conversation will become increasingly available to meet the problems of our time.

There is an irony in the fact that the attention being given to the method of Group Conversation is a result of the urban conflicts and racial tensions that are placing their stamp upon this decade. For forty years Rachel Davis DuBois, who originated the method, has understood that it would finally be in the area of intergroup relations that the concept of American democracy would meet its fundamental test. In the years when questions of racial conflict had not yet reached the point of ultimate confrontation, she developed an approach that was soft and, if not altogether painless, often quite pleasant. It was an approach that drew people together by reaching into their differences and touching at a deep emotional level the common ground of their humanness.

Her conception in those early years was that if enough Americans would work to achieve a mutuality of dialogue on this level, the infection of racial conflict would never need to fester. But, as is the case with most persons who see ahead of their time, the opportunity which she gave this country to take a major step forward toward full cultural democracy was hardly accepted. A crisis was required before the meaning and the value of her conception could be grasped. We have come to that crisis now, and that is why the methods of Group Conversation are being increasingly called upon.

9

I have said that Group Conversation takes a "soft" approach to groups. It is soft in the sense that it is not abrasive in the way that the "confrontation" and "anger-expression" approaches to group work often are. But softness is a quality that is full of surprises. It has amazing powers. Since I first read of it many years ago, I have often found myself thinking about the observation made by Lao Tse that water is the softest of substances, for anything can push water out of the way. And yet water has the power to erode the hardest rocks. There is something of that soft power in the attitude of mind that underlies the method of Group Conversation. One finds it also in the quality of love and steadfastness with which Rachel DuBois has nurtured the method over the decades. Mew-Soong Li's particular contribution has been to open the way to deeper experiences and, through the use of additional techniques, to extend the impact of such experiences. Group Conversation has much to give, and it insists on making its contribution. Increasingly we have reason to be glad that it is here.

What does Group Conversation do? Essentially it draws people together where there were differences between them keeping them apart. The differences may be for any reason—racial, religious, cultural, temperamental. Group Conversation does not try to resolve the differences. It does not try to alter them. And yet it contributes toward an atmosphere of harmony that overcomes conflict by placing it in a new light, and opens the door to resolving the causes of the conflict.

I gratefully remember my experiences in leading Group Conversations with Rachel DuBois and Mew Li some years ago. Those experiences provided me with basic insights into group differences and the ways of overcoming them. In those groups the participants were of very different backgrounds and of divergent points of view. We did not try to by-pass those differences, however; neither did we try to resolve them. We just let them be there, be stated, felt, and shared. To do that seemed to have a very great force in and of itself.

In leading those groups we would place a neutral question before the group, usually a question that turned the focus of thought back to the years of childhood. I remember one especially dramatic session we had that began in a deceptively mild and innocent way. We simply asked the participants in a workshop at a multiracial and multinational housing project to recall the experiences they had

had around Christmastime when they were about ten years of age. The depths of emotion that were evoked by that simple question were a tremendous experience to me and taught me much about the dynamics and possibilities of group work.

What took place was elemental. Each person told his own experience, felt it himself, and felt it being shared by others. Each person spoke out of the uniqueness of his own experience. Each merely told the memory, and since it was a memory of days long past, it was neutral to them. It was beyond praise or blame, beyond being proud of or being ashamed of. They simply told their memory, each out of his own cultural, national, racial background. Each spoke out of his differences, and thereby implicitly accepted these differences. In effect, the Group Conversation brought them all down to the common denominator of their humanness. At that level of experience, human beings cannot help but feel love for one another. The trouble is that most modern ideologies and group methods take people not down into the well where love is but out onto the surface where anger thrives.

I see Group Conversation as having a major contribution to make to the modern situation in two specific ways. The first is its capacity to overcome racial and cultural conflicts by drawing individuals to a loving acceptance of one another's differences. As young people of all ages would say nowadays, it is "beautiful" to be present and participating when that happens in the experience of a Group Conversation.

The second contribution lies in something even deeper that Group Conversation brings about. When people share the intimate memories of their lives, they not only affirm one another's differences and the right of each and every human being to exist in his own uniqueness, but they awaken in themselves a slumbering awareness of their still unopened potentials, and an intimation of the spiritual magnitudes that are contained in being a human being.

For such persons, the experience of Group Conversation leads beyond itself. It leads the individual to a new type of journey and exploration of his inner experiences. Especially Group Conversation opens the way to further and deeper experiences and an ability to use additional techniques.

I can speak of it best from my own personal experience. A number of years ago Group Conversation opened an awareness for me of the depth of personality available through group procedures. I therefore consider Rachel DuBois and the method of Group Conversation to be the primary source for my later developments in group workshop procedures, especially the Intensive Journal method that is used in the Dialogue House program for the development of persons. For this, I am tremendously and lovingly grateful.

IRA PROGOFF

Dialogue House
New York City
May, 1970

Introduction

Literally hundreds of thousands of adult and young adult men and women in the United States, and in all countries, are brought together in thousands of groupings: informal and formal; *ad hoc,* transient, temporary, emergency; social, civic, cultural, economic, business, political, religious, ethnic, fraternal, veteran, patriotic, "cause" promoting, and many more, including myriad combinations of these forms.

Such groupings are so characteristic of modern society that we rarely sort them out. They are as commonplace as the workaday gathering of men and women in an office or industrial plant; school or college faculty; hospital or library staff; boards and committees of churches and synagogues; committees guiding civic groups and youth-serving agencies; municipal, state and federal bodies; recreation commissions; union and labor-management groups; trade associations, and so on.

In recent years, less common groups have been organized to bring together people, often strangers to one another (who are approaching conflict or have sensed it), to reduce and hopefully to end the tensions which, if unresolved, precipitate hostility and conflict. In other cases, men and women have been brought together where there was little, if any tension—only separation and alienation—to build co-operation and to reach specific goals of direct benefit to the members of the groups.

The recent proliferation of such *ad hoc* groups has often been inspired and sometimes financed by governmental agencies, such as the Office of Economic Opportunity, VISTA and overseas by the

13

U.S. Agency for International Development and the Peace Corps. In some outstanding instances, private foundations and large corporations have also furnished direction and finances for such groups. Typically, groups formed by such bodies are community-based and bring together disparate elements to work toward common goals. Under government, social agency or private aegis, other *ad hoc* groups have been formed to ease racial tensions, again for the most part on a community basis.

It is largely, though not entirely, with these *ad hoc* groups that Group Conversation has been applied most frequently, as case histories in this manual indicate.

But at some time or times in their existence—most often at the time of each new formation—the "permanent" groups which we cited initially experience person-to-person tensions which may range from mild and transitory to grave conflicts that jeopardize the goals and continued life of the organization. The Group Conversation method can be applied effectively at any point within the range of tension in these "permanent" groups—ideally, of course, in the early stages before the tension can fester into disruptive conflict.

Group Conversation was created for the leaders and the members of all these groups in society. Unlike most other methods of opening channels of communication between strangers or foes, Group Conversation is accessible to a leader, with or without professional training in the behavioral and social sciences. The techniques are learned easily, mostly because they are so natural. Perhaps one of its greatest virtues is that even when conducted by a person with little training in group leadership but with considerable experience in the use of the method, Group Conversation does not carry seeds of dissension.

Group Conversation, in short, is almost universally utilizable, in thousands of settings and situations, and with all kinds of people. Even in its minimal achievements, such as in single brief sessions without follow-up, Group Conversation has been found pragmatically to move groups forward in mutual understanding, compassion and communication . . . never backward, never leaving them at status quo.

Group Conversation is for the leaders and members of all groups, as well as for the dispassionate "outsider" with experience in the method who is often best received as the trainer and initiator of the process.

Unknowingly, thousands of Group Conversation participants here and abroad have enriched this book. Our special thanks go to Miss Bernice Cofer for her insightful guidance and to the Lucius N. Littauer Foundation in the preparation of the manuscript.

PART I

THE ART

1

What Is Group Conversation?

WAR, POVERTY, RACISM. These are no longer submerged issues about which most keep silent, if with a shrug. In these revolutionary times they evoke an activism that translates instantly into a sleep-in, a draft card bonfire, a prayer vigil, or a march on the White House. Furthermore such nonviolent acts of civil disobedience often flare now into volatile mob events—burning and rioting, if not tragic occasions for self-immolation.

However we elect to deny or withdraw from these circumstances, there is no longer escape from their impingement on our daily transactions with life. No citizen is absolved from their consequences; no child protected from their destructive, disturbing, detribalizing impact. Concomitant drug abuse, crime, distrust and disillusion spare too few.

The despair induced by the disorientation and dislocation develops soon into hostility and loss of faith. Communication channels among the many disparate elements that mount quickly in a community at odds with itself become drastically reduced at a time when open minds are most necessary to unify efforts towards constructive, deliberate action.

Few American communities are not directly affected by these dynamics. They assume different structural specifics, but the psychological impact of the circumstances takes on a similar cast. The

19

result is such an assault on the elements and resources of a particular aggregation as often to lead to a paralyzing inability in the group to deal with the problems which ensue.

Common Person-to-Person Tensions That Confront Us

Situations such as the following confront communities across our land:

—Parents and teachers in a newly-desegrated school who cannot come together leave their youngsters vulnerable to hostile action and the ravages of hate. *How can we build constructive co-operative action where two centuries of ignorance and discrimination have done their worst?*

—Adults are helpless, frustrated because they cannot reach their children. The generation gap is so wide today that the chasm seems insurmountable. *How can we help them find what they have in common so they can proceed to satisfying relationships?*

—Government anti-poverty programs insist that the consumer population have more of a participatory and decision-making role. *How can we reach dissident elements on a level that will lay the ground for a cross-community base for the development of community action agencies?*

—Community organizations are unable to find volunteers whose help they need today because of changed social considerations or because some groups have not usually been reached. *Where and how can we look for them? motivate them?*

—Americans are moving into new neighborhoods, many created by new housing programs. Relationships are potentially good or bad. *What kind of preparation for full intergroup living is needed, and can leadership for it be developed?*

—Labor leaders, especially in Southern shops, know that members of both races must work together harmoniously in their unions. Interracial communication is almost zero. *How can this be overcome?*

—The Kerner report assures us that peaceful demonstration for dissent is a civil right, but violence is often started by the onlookers. *How can we assure less explosive and more constructive action?*

—"Head Start" parents often do not accept each other or their role in programs for their young children. *How can we help develop closer concern for the total family and the full community, and implement it?*

—Many businessmen say they want to give employment to "hard-core youths." *What kind of training is needed to bring about mutual responsibility and a real chance to develop new careers?*

—Campus dissent is at a volatile high. *How can faculty and authorities be more responsive to the legitimate grievances of students? How can this be accomplished with sensitivity to the needs and concerns of the new generation without depriving them of the opportunity to make their own decisions and without losing their respect and love?*

—Poverty and oversized families seem to go hand in hand. To overcome the first, it is important that low-income families have free access to information and services to reduce potential family size. *How can we achieve this in the most sensitive, effective way?*

How can we transcend exacerbating circumstances so that the community can experience some redemptive healing relationship for those who live and work in the area? There is need for approaches that are fresh, renewing, creative, where heart can reach out to human heart in joy and love.

What are some of the individual differences which become blocks to group development and barriers to organizational or community leaders in their endeavors to keep or build a sense of community in these chaotic times? We all know these blocks. They are the differences in age, race, social status, ethnic background, religious faith, sometimes regions, economic income, and educational sophistication.

Detailed reports of group experiences in which many of these blocks were removed because differences came to be seen as assets will be found throughout this book. We offer here from our experience a manual on how to lead a Group Conversation, how the leader can adapt it to his particular social action goal, and how he can use it with other group methods in order to get maximum results from such time as he spends in groups.

A Widely Tested Method That Works

For some years the authors of this book have been working with groups and communities looking for ways to attack such problems or to deal with feelings about them when answers were not readily forthcoming. In hundreds of groups such questions have been raised many times over in different ways and in various contexts—some more profound, more complex, more direct than others. Some solutions have been less relevant, less complete, less direct than others. Generally, however, they have reawakened attributes and abilities of the persons gathered, bringing to the group's deliberations and concerns such resources and energies as to make their experience together a meaningful one. This is to say that the way toward a solution is usually illuminated with a new sense of mutual trust and discovery of new insights about oneself. About each other. About the group. About getting together on the problem. About renewal. This restructuring of the situation to bring a wholeness of the group focused upon a particular concern, we see as a key for the group to use in dealing with problems which our society has allowed to alienate us as persons, as people, as communities, as a nation.

There are, then, many reasons for the use of Group Conversation by the alert group worker. Among these reasons are:

(1) To help make for an easier access one to another just as persons, without the socio-economic trappings and status that so often block direct communication.

(2) To help leaders to become more aware of their own feelings and be more sensitive to the feelings and needs of others.

(3) To help counteract stereotyped attitudes often found among members of various racial, religious and cultural groups, and by releasing the potential mutual enrichment in such groupings to promote understanding among and active interest in them, leading to a richer common American life.

(4) To cultivate among all members of an organization, new and old, a deeper sense of belonging and fellowship.

(5) To integrate the newcomer, the person from another ethnic group, the student from abroad, the refugee, the member of another generation, the migrant worker, and so on, into the fellowship of the group.

The Unique Qualities of Group Conversation

When a small number of persons—from 10 to at most 30—take an hour in which to exchange memories of experiences of joy or sorrow in a group experience based on spontaneity, a warmth and closeness develop quietly and quickly. When this sharing is directed around a universal theme, even a very mixed group can see and feel the oneness of the human family and can gain an appreciation of the beauty, significance and wondrous qualities inherent in diversity.

Group Conversation is this face-to-face sharing of experiences both of the past and of the present in a spontaneous atmosphere which quickly produces rapport. This kind of sharing helps to break down the fears and suspicions that separate us because our culture has taught us to see our differences of age, race, ethnicity, creed or class as liabilities. While the initial phases of the give-and-take in a Group Conversation are not problem-centered, they help build a basis of faith and trust upon which the participants can more effectively work out their problems of living together in home and community. This is the uniqueness of Group Conversation— its ability to quickly produce confidence and trust among its participants.

The method described in this book seeks to change the group situation in such a way as to transcend the fear, suspicion and hostility so that these forces do not stand in the way of our dealing positively with them as they arise in our day-to-day transactions with life. The process we call Group Conversation is a way of using a group to center on each of its members and a way of helping its members to develop into a real group. Its impact on the individual helps him become more sensitive to life's moments and often to motivate him to bring about needed change, both within himself and within his environment. It is the kind of change which brings deeper, more sincere and satisfying communication between individuals and thereby gives a richer quality to our common American life.

In training workshops the authors of this book have shared this group skill with many others in various parts of this country and abroad. They have found that Group Conversation can be quickly learned and practiced by group leaders in community centers, government agencies, schools, teacher training institutions, churches, and even in homes. They also know that our present crises demand new applications of this method. These new applications, used alone or with other group methods, have been evolved since 1963 when our first manual was published.

Psychological Roots of Group Conversation's Success

Group Conversation is a way of helping members of a group to experience a sense of our common humanity by first reaching back into the past for memorable experiences to be shared around a topic of universal moment. The method is designed to facilitate real and spontaneous communication by developing the social climate which fosters mutual regard and confidence.

Leaders in social psychology and group procedures see Group Conversation as a unique and important step in the development of the group, and many have commented on the effectiveness of this simple informal method for quickly establishing rapport. Participants are brought into greater readiness for encounter, discussion, problem solving, decision making, and other levels of social thinking and action. Because it breaks through to the unifying feelings, Group Conversation leads to the kind of communication that reaches the heart of a human situation.

Dr. Gordon Allport after experiencing the process said, "The participant does not think himself into a democratic way of acting (as lecturers, preachers, and writers ask us to do) but rather *acts* himself into a democratic way of thinking. This is sound psychology."

Group Conversation Revives a Lost Art

We have called this particular process Group Conversation because that is what it is—conversation in the setting of a group. Like any other good conversation form, that much lamented lost art, it requires a willingness to share and a willingness to listen creatively with tenderness and firmness.

Understanding and real communication can come only in wholeness and freedom. If we reflect on these attributes, we realize that they are requisite to all human relationships, of which person-to-person conversation is a highly developed and yet spontaneous form.

Spontaneity is of the essence, and a well-conducted session can be a moving and profound experience. This seeming paradox implies a delicate balance of trust and expectation. It requires that the leader not only be open to all the magic that can be touched off in a group, but that he be alert as well to catch the sparks that can set it off. It means that he must be able to convey this faith and sense of ease to the group; but, as with any art, this ability comes with practice. The leader learns to be spontaneous and to trust the group because time and time again something comes spontaneously from the group which is so much more moving than anything he may have thought of during his planning. In fact, he learns so much from the group—gets such a sense of self-fulfillment and inspiration—that sometimes he uses the phrase, "There is magic in a group." At least he can offer the hypothesis that there is a spirit below the verbal level which includes us all—a spirit which, as it begins to flow in the group, seems to be trying all over the world today to break through our individual crusts to let us know there *is* a reality in which we are all one.

This unifying feeling is so necessary to the strength of a group that all group leaders might well consider using regularly some method to produce (or, shall we say, release) this feeling of belonging together. In the most dangerous phase of the civil rights struggle in the South no march or demonstration ever took place without spending at least an hour's time in singing freedom songs. The leaders knew the time was well spent, for it was this feeling which carried and upheld them in facing electric prods, dogs, clubs and even jail. The Religious Society of Friends uses the unifying process of a period of group silence not only in the hour-long weekly Meeting for Worship, but also before and after every committee meeting or monthly Meeting for Business. If this unifying feeling of identity with each other is lost during the discussion in any group when some particularly difficult issue has arisen, the art of Group Conversation can well be used to establish a sense of unity which may work through a deadlock in discussion.

An Example of Group Conversation in Action

Probably the most effective way to illustrate how Group Conversation can work is to offer this report of one Group Conversation among the thousands which have happened:

A Southern union was opening its doors for Negro membership, but there was little communication between blacks and whites. Knowing the restraint, even hostility, of their white fellow workers, blacks rarely attended union meetings. Sensing that what was needed was to have union members engage in encounter groups along with Group Conversation, the union's regional director arranged a weekend in the country near a Georgia village for 46 black and white factory workers from seven different unions. It was hoped that the participants would come away from the weekend with a sense of personal growth and mutual acceptance.

At the start a few white women, when they realized they had to sleep in the same dormitory with blacks, were quite hostile and wanted to go home at once. However, they agreed to attend the memories around food experiences. Among other foods, fried ham for breakfast was a common memory, for most of the participants had been brought up on farms. "Where did we get the ham from in those days?" "Hog killings," came the answer, "the day that neighbors helped each other." The way the adults killed the animals was vividly described—the shootings, the cutting of throats, even the squealing of the pigs came back vividly in memory.

"How did we feel as children watching this?" "We couldn't stand it." Both Negroes and whites used the same gestures, covering their faces with their hands, when they recalled the traumatic experiences. "Yes, that is a universal childhood feeling," said the leader. "I'd like to paraphrase a thought from Gibran's prophet: 'If in order to eat, you must kill a beast, say to him in your heart that you too are slain, that you too are consumed.'" There was a deep and unifying silence. This was finally broken by the group's spontaneously singing "Let Us Break Bread Together on Our Knees."

Then the leader asked what kind of grace was said at the tables around this food. Several remembered a common one: "Bless this food to our use and us to Thy service." The relation of this to the line from Gibran was clear. The session ended with the group singing the grace which the Fisk Jubilee Singers sang around the world soon after the Civil War:

Thou art great
And Thou art good

And we thank Thee
For this food
By Thy hand must all be fed
Give us now our daily bread.

By now much of the initial feeling of hostility was gone. One of the twelve white women who had wanted to go home said she was glad she had stayed: "I would not have missed this meeting for the world." The unifying experience of Group Conversation was used twice more during the weekend of encountering.

After experiencing their common feelings around some universal topic—in this case, food—the participants now had enough mutual confidence and trust to be able to bear the thrust of honesty and challenge of an encounter group even when voices were raised and harsh things said. One white woman said in such an encounter, "I grew up in Alabama and I was taught to hate and fear black people." This was followed by a cry from several Negroes, "Why? Why?" The white woman answered quietly, "I never knew you were like this."

At one point a union leader turned to her heretofore unco-operative black counterpart and asked for cooperation in their union work back home. While not all hostility was overcome in one weekend, the feedback from the several unions represented showed more cooperation on back-home problems between those who had participated in the weekend encounter groups.

This experience shows how a roomful of people, even strangers with varied backgrounds, can be helped to feel something of the warmth and trust of long-time neighbors and friends. This Group Conversation session was aimed at helping to start flowing in a group that spirit of mutual confidence and trust needed when members enter later an encounter group which by its nature consists of being honest even if it hurts. Very often encounter groups, starting first with expressions of anger, end on a note of anger with less than a sense of growth. We have briefly related here what happened in the group in order to help the reader see some of the dynamics in the group process—the development of the kind of give-and-take which is central to Group Conversation.

2

Group Conversation Enhances
Other Methods

WHILE SOMETIMES Group Conversation is used alone as an enriching, esthetic, even an entertaining social experience in itself * to
help a group reach its goals of social action more easily and effectively, it is most often used in connection with other group methods.
How this is done and its values for enhancing the effectiveness of
the other group methods will be seen more clearly as we explore
its use in these pages.

When we think of steps in the total group process as proceeding
from getting acquainted to group discussion, to group decision, and
finally to group action and individual commitment to that action,
then we can see that Group Conversation can in many instances be
a first experience. But this method is more than an ice breaker,
more than merely getting to know the names of those who have
come together and a briefly-told fact about them. Those who have
used Group Conversation as it is meant to be used (for instance,
before discussion of a problem) know that the time is well spent.

* For a further exposition of this use of Group Conversation, see *Get Together Americans* by Rachel Davis DuBois (New York, Harper & Bros.,
1943).

Its influence is felt in all the other steps of the total process; thus both time and energy are saved.

Facilitates Group Discussion

Group Conversation is not group discussion but moves into it when relevant. Group Conversation purposefully uses a minimum of structuring of the group so that discussion of problems is not invited at the outset of a meeting. The controversial aspects of an issue are intentionally postponed until a mood of acceptance has been developed so that the members of the group are able to enter the discussion phase when they are ready to enter into it constructively and with a sense of trust, openness and directness. On one occasion a militant black youth came to a teacher-student group session with the intent of "telling it like it is" at the very start. He was assured by the leader while introducing the process, that discussion would come later. By the time the black youth had shared some of his childhood experiences in a ghetto school and neighborhood and had listened to the experiences of others (some similar to his, others different), a feeling of mutual acceptance had been released, with the result that, with anger dissipated, the youth after coffee gave the kind of moving and challenging word picture of life in the ghetto that those middle-class teachers, both Negro and white, needed to hear.

Most experienced leaders know that, until the feeling of strangeness, suspicion or even hostility is cleared, little real business in any meeting can be taken care of. When the feelings are complicated by many kinds of differences, not to mention those of nationality, religion or race, the blocks to real group development can be serious.

If we assume that a group goes from discussion to problem solving and decision, thence to commitment and action, then Group Conversation may be seen as a prior step to this progression. Group Conversation prepares for profitable discussion by helping to point up the basic and strategic aspects of a problem so that the group can look squarely at what is the issue, then get to work on it. Too often we cover up what is fundamental by cluttering the issue with nonessentials; we lose sight of the goals of a program or the crux of a problem. We consciously and purposely hide certain crucial data from others, or unconsciously secrete them from ourselves.

Here is where Group Conversation can be especially helpful; it can bring up to the level of awareness much of the material which we, either as individuals or as a group, have pushed below with our rationalizations.

Sharing earlier experiences of having been made to feel strange or different or queer, or of being rejected or of rejecting, may, for example, bring important facets and depth to the exploration of some aspect of the fair employment or school integration issues. The kind of data we should need to look for, how we could best go about getting at them—in fact, the very way we formulate a problem—could be uncovered by the kind of interchange at this level of emotional involvement.

The discussion phase may flow directly out of concerns pointed up in the Group Conversation and become one continuous process if the leader feels at home in both techniques. Or the discussion may follow a coffee or refreshment break.

The topic for the Group Conversation need not necessarily be related to the problem to be discussed, though often it is. A meeting between white and black men who are real estate operators, meeting together for the first time to consider first steps they might take toward open housing in a Southern city, matched their memories of boyhood games at the start of the evening. The release of tensions through laughter about those early escapades, and they were very similar as they were all American boys, gave the group the momentum after coffee to make some first steps together on the thorny subject of housing.

Another Group Conversation illustrating this point took place in a Chicago suburb where the town council had been discussing ways to make it possible for more moderate– and low–income families to move into the area. An integrated group met in a clergyman's home. Before coffee the Group Conversation leader asked them, by way of getting acquainted, to share their early work memories. One of the Negro men (five black families had already moved into the area) matched or rather contrasted with white men his experiences of selling papers as a ten-year-old in the slums of South Chicago. "I knew what went on in those saloons at midnight." The others in the group identified with him asking friendly questions. To one, he answered, "The first thing I bought with my money was my first pair of shoes. Sneakers can get pretty cold on city streets in the winter."

When he was asked why he had moved to this suburb he replied, "My sister worked here, and then she moved here. I could not at first, understand how she could stand not being near all the people and places we were used to. And then when I came out of the army and the hospital, I stayed here with her some weeks. It was then for the first time in my life that I realized what being with trees and flowers and grass and the wide-open sky can do for people. I want no child of mine to grow up where I did."

The group discussion, which followed the coffee break, through using sociological and political hard facts connected with the housing problem could develop the necessary motivation and commitment to move the group into action because it was able to get down to the real dimensions of any housing problem—the people who work and play and live in the physical structures that shelter and nurture their love and growth as families.

Sometimes the Group Conversation used before discussion draws off enough hostility and anger to enable the faculties of reason and analysis necessary for discussion to function.

Group Conversation serves as a prelude to the workshop. It establishes an atmosphere that inspires the participants to share the kind of experiences that will bring deeper meaning to the impact of the total workshop. A busy industrial leader, given a chance to reminisce on his early rivalry with an older brother, may suddenly be helped to see the need for along-the-line decision-making in his factory work situation. A teacher recalling an early unfortunate classroom encounter in her first term as a student may be made more sensitive to the needs of her pupils.

Impetus to Conference Progress

For introducing the theme of a conference, seminar, or workshop, Group Conversation can be very effective. It can help a group, meeting for the first time, and for a short period, to move into the matter at hand much more rapidly and directly. Not only can the necessary details of introduction be taken care of, but attendant anxieties to establish identity and "protocol" (a need so much more pronounced in the frenzy and briefness of conference encounters) can be allayed. Members are more ready to buckle down to business, in sufficient depth to proceed with intensity and progress. Many leaders who have worked a Group Conversation into the schedule find that the time is more than compensated for by the speed with which the rest of the meeting moves into the heart of the discussion and action.

There may be occasion to use several group methods with Group Conversation. As an initial event on any program, Group Conversation can be valuable for the reasons given above. It may be used at any time in a schedule to open up a session, or a discussion, or a new structuring of the group.

If the assembly is a large one, the different units may be set up in a concurrent round of Group Conversations. A skilled leader can work with a very large group, but should not look for as deep penetration in the individual experiences. Through vicarious participation, however, a group mood can be developed even in a large gathering which carries over into other parts of the program. If the conference is on urban renewal and housing, for example, a Group Conversation, carefully planned to elicit emotional experiences around home or rooms with which we can identify deeply, can be a potent discussion dynamic.

Provides Warm-up for Buzz Groups

Group Conversation can be used very effectively to warm up a large group preparatory to its break-up into buzz groups in which case real thought must go into structuring the questions that are to be buzzed. The leader should be reminded also that the dividing of the groups should be done as quickly and easily as possible. The questions may be the same for all the groups, or they may follow a split into whatever areas of differentiation have been planned. They should, however, enhance or sharpen the areas of personal as well as group relevance and identity. For example, if the topic is "Adult and Teenage Relations," questions to be considered should directly tease out most recent firsthand experiences with a teenager or an adult, as the case may be.

In a recent weekend conference on rebellion in the high schools, made up of parents, teachers and teenagers, the initial Group Conversation moved the adults to concede that they too had rebelled when they were in school or college. Even though social conditions were not as serious then as now, the courage to rebel is of the same quality whether in a large or small frame. In one such group the oldsters had rebelled against the sweatshop conditions of their youth and several had helped to organize a union. In such conferences youth and age learn much from each other.

Sets Up Role Play

For the leader who is trained in role playing and can see applicable incidents to play out for elucidation or for psycho- or socio-dramatic impact, Group Conversation is a particularly fertile source for this kind of material, easier and more relevant to deal with than incidents imagined before the session by the role play leader. Here, the experience to be re-enacted, with the full potential and range of role playing, is oftentimes the more dramatic and meaningful because it arises in the context of the group's sharing and situation.

The Group Conversation leader need not be the one to stage the role playing. Often it would be well for the two functions to be lodged in different persons, especially if both are sensitive to group phenomena and to each other's leadership style. Perhaps for those new to the method, it would be better for the role playing to follow the completion of the Group Conversation phase. It may not be easy for the novice to keep hold of the mood or direction of the Group Conversation although, by and large, both processes operate on the dimensions of the emotions. As one familiar with the dynamics and procedures of role playing is aware, the closer to the evaluation of the experience the re-enactment can come, the greater the psychological impact. However, because the incident is the emotional property of the group, it can be used with effect at any time in the context of the group. Hence, until the Group Conversation leader develops confidence and competency, it may be well to let it come as a separate event in the program.

The experienced leader of role playing will see that its use in the context discussed is especially effective in problems of social or self-inquiry and understanding. Where the group is small and is an ongoing one, it is very often effective to play out the incident as it is offered in the Group Conversation, in any or all of the ramifications that may ensue in role playing. This is especially true in a psycho-dramatic situation. The trained Group Conversation leader can then pick up again and move on through to the next step in the development of the session.

Very often we have found that the playing out of a highly relevant experience becomes the moving and impact-filled climax of a meeting. It becomes, that is, the dramatic ending of the Group Conversation session. The sensitive leader will know when this happens and will be guided by the response of the group. Whether the group moves from this point depends on its resources, needs, and maturity as a group, and on the awareness, imagination, and creativity of its leaders.

In a measure, this attests to the flexibility of Group Conversation as a social instrument. It also points to the potency of well used group resources when leader and participants feel secure and trustful enough to invest themselves fully and freely in the group. The fullness of the moment can be translated into many kinds of assets on which can be built dimensions of growth as an individual, as a group, as a community, as a people.

Used with Other Methods

I

SITUATION. A weekend retreat conference on school integration, convened in the Catskill Mountains for thirty-two white and black teachers from one county in New York State.

AUSPICES. The Dialogue Department of the Southern Christian Leadership Conference and the Race Relations Committee of the New York Yearly Meeting of the Religious Society of Friends.

GOALS OF THE CONFERENCE. To develop communication between Negro and white teachers at a deep and meaningful level. To help each other understand some of their pupils' feelings which are not shared across racial barriers. To identify and overcome some of those barriers in the lives of teachers, students and parents. If possible to set a pattern for future conferences with similar goals.

GROUP METHODS USED. *Group Conversation.* By beginning the conference at a level where all might enter on an equal footing, Group Conversation was used to invoke the sharing of memories involving the frustrations and aspirations of the participants' school days. Group Conversation was also used at the end of the conference, asking the educators to explore the topic, "My Journey as a Teacher." *Work groups.* By providing a one-to-one relationship (racially balanced) for ample communication during free time following stimulating joint activities (working together on the conference grounds), participants were led to discover that they could think and feel and laugh together. *Panel discussion.* Teachers, administrators and parents were selected to comprise a panel that discussed basic problems of school integration in yet another dimension. *Conference evaluation.*

SESSION ONE. Group Conversation around the topic, "School Days," was used initially to stimulate and deepen communication among the participants, and to set the tone of the conference. *Lead questions included:* Who was the teacher who inspired and helped you most? Was there a teacher who was unjust to you, and perhaps closed doors to your mind? Did you rebel? If so, how?

As early school memories were revived, many remembered that they had felt rebellious. Some recalled at least one teacher with a vivid sense of rage. But these memories were offset by recollections of other teachers who had inspired them, had had faith in their abilities, and had opened new vistas for them.

To lead the participants to apply these remembrances to the problems confronting them in their school setting today, a final question was posed: Do the memories of your own rebellion help you to understand some aspects of the student rebellion today?

SESSION TWO. The panel discussion following the Group Conversation centered on the theme of "School Integration and Frustrations," and was conducted by a racially mixed group of teachers, administrators and parents. *Typical excerpts from the panel discussion follow.*

A white teacher: "I'm a fourth-grade teacher. Must I drag in by its coattails Negro history where it doesn't belong just because everybody is talking about it now?"

An administrator: "Perhaps we principals should be more alert when we hire teachers to see if they know facts like that, facts which make us know the strength of our cultural diversity. Then no teacher would feel she had to 'drag it in' because it would be integrated into her teaching as a part of the total picture."

A black teacher: "How can we help change the social atmosphere of a school when some teachers say, 'What's going to happen to this school when *those* people come into it?' It's always 'those'! Our Negro children can *feel* that attitude."

The administrator admitted that this condition could be over-come if an integrated faculty could feel and say "us."

A Negro mother: "With three boys in school, my frustrations are especially great. I'm so confused—some tell me to push my chil-dren, and some say not to. I suppose my frustration is partly caused by my own image of the school as that place where they did *me* in. The teacher of my son only calls me when there is a problem, and then long after it has become a problem. Yet at the PTA meeting the month before, she had been nice and formal. When I asked her about my boy, she had said, 'He's okay.'

"And my other boy—I pay for his private music lessons. He's so good at it he now wants a thousand-dollar piano. But the school!!! They don't even know he loves music. Why can't the school give our children some praise, some recognition so they'll feel they *are* something?

"I know some of us parents are too pushy. But it's because we don't feel a part of you, and we know what our kids have got to go through. If you white teachers who are friendly would work with us in the NAACP or some other county group, then we could all work together. But sometimes I feel like I'll go back home and lock the door and never come out again!"

Another black parent: "I'm frustrated because too many Negro children enter classrooms already prejudged by the teachers as to both the capability of the youngster and his performance. Many times, failure is already assumed. They don't discuss the black child's learning problems with his parents like they do with white parents.

"Another cause of frustration is that when we attempt to talk honestly about the problems, the white teachers tend to think we are 'too threatening' or 'oversensitive,' and that we tend to see things that aren't there."

SESSION THREE. After lunch, the work groups met for further free discussion. *A participant reported:*

"We talked about practical things we can do in our classrooms. This discussion was led by the specialist in intercultural education from the State Department [of Education]. She made many helpful suggestions as she described the many school-community projects in process in different parts of the state, or in the planning stage. She had brought several booklets on new and pertinent curriculum practices which can be secured for the asking. 'But,' she reminded us, 'there is no substitute for the kind of experiences you're having this weekend.' "

SESSION FOUR—CONFERENCE EVALUATION. Participants were encouraged to summarize their reactions to the weekend events. *Significant comments of two of the white teachers follow.*

"We white teachers have fears also, not only about being good teachers, but of losing our jobs or status as Negroes move in. Having honest confrontations with them, as we are here, helps us to accept them and go on. Growth can come through the negative also."

"I've never communicated," said another white teacher, "or perhaps I should say, never taken an opportunity to communicate deeply with any Negro parent, or even with a fellow teacher who is black. But this weekend has made me aware of what I have been missing."

A black teacher then observed: "Some of the people who needed to be here are going to pick softer spots to teach in—with people like themselves with whom it is easier to communicate. Our experiences here have been mainly in the nature of *feeling* and cannot be communicated. We should provide the same kind of experience for those teachers."

OUTCOME. The teachers, on their own initiative, proposed carrying on the work begun there, and set a date for another gathering three weeks later. Said one of the teachers: "We must do all we can to keep our newly made contacts—perhaps inviting each other to our Saturday evenings with other friends and neighbors, besides seeing each other in our more formal professional meetings."

II

SITUATION. A one-day conference on black-white polarization and the generation gap in public education, convened at Powell House, Old Chatham, N.Y., for a black-white group of high school students, parents, teachers and school administrators.

AUSPICES. The New York Yearly Meeting of the Religious Society of Friends.

GOALS OF THE CONFERENCE. To bridge not only the black-white gap but also the generation gap—both of which divide parents and children, and teachers and students.

GROUP METHODS USED. Group Conversation, panel discussion, work groups, conference evaluation. (All sessions were tape recorded, with the knowledge of the participants.)

PROGRAM. Topics included: school decentralization, community control; curriculum changes; pressures on teachers and administrators; charges of racism and anti-Semitism; selection and policies of boards of education.

SESSION ONE. The Group Conversation topic, "Rebellion—Then and Now," was initiated with these *lead questions:*

Who was the authority figure in your home? Who did the punishing? What particular incident do you recall of receiving just or unjust punishment? How did you feel? Did anyone wish to, or actually, run away from home? Did you rebel in any other way?

What about school—pleasant? unpleasant? What memories of your 'best' teacher? Why? What memories of your 'worst' teacher? Why? Did you rebel at school? In what ways? What, if any, were the results?

Some significant comments of the participants follow.

"When I was in college, we couldn't make any decisions for ourselves. Another girl and I rebelled—we broke all the rules and spent the whole night out of the dormitory. Later, our class was responsible for the first student government in that college."

"I, too, left college. It was in Texas. I struck out for the West."

"Not knowing enough to make decisions at that time" was voiced by both age levels.

"Sometimes the wisdom of an oldster can help, but once I was let down by an older person."

"The difference between the rebellion of a generation ago and that of today is that it is closer to a social revolution today."

The leader summarized: "We see that our experiences have been similar, and yet we feel the age barrier. Will it help to stand, and oldsters and youngsters put hands on each other's shoulders, and look into the eyes of the other person until we feel there isn't an awful lot of difference?"

SESSION TWO. A panel discussion on the topic, "How Is Today's Revolution Being Expressed in High Schools?," evoked these reactions among the panelists.

"In our school a black students' assembly grew into a big fracas. Police were called in, and three students were charged with assault."

Students from four other schools reported intergroup tension. "What is the cause of this unrest in our schools?" the panelists were asked. "Black students feel left out; they see what's happening in the adult world, in ghettos and in colleges. So they want equal rights in high school, and they won't wait."

At this point, a teacher on the panel role-played the devil's advocate, showing the tenor of white backlash. Finally the "What do they want" question was firmly answered: "The same as anybody else—justice and equal opportunity." "And we all want more power to decide our own destiny." "Boy, every time I opened my mouth I ended up in the principal's office. The teacher had power; I didn't." "Students have been playing an important role in Vietnam, yet we see adults talk one way and act another." "We want a social revolution, an end of the military-industrial complex."

In the discussion summary, the panel leader observed: "We seem to be in a real movement in our high schools, a gut reaction to a social system which students hate. Their frustration is coming out now; much of it is spontaneous, without organization."

SESSION THREE. *Work groups offered these specifics for high schools:* More flexible, relevant curriculum. Remedial courses. Qualified teachers, black and white. Co-op programs, including projects with common black and white goals. Smaller classes. Controversial speakers and reading. Specialized high schools. Teachers from the ghetto, despite their present exclusion by "high educational standards."

Further recommendations: Draft counseling. Student involvement in written evaluations of teachers' work before granting tenure. Civil liberties for students. Parents as school aides. Co-ed sex education, including facts on planned parenthood. End of corporal punishment, physical force, and military atmosphere in school. End of censorship. End of Regents examinations [standardized statewide tests in several major subject areas, devised and check-scored by the N.Y. State Department of Education]. End of grades. Abolition of school zoning—and the ghetto.

Some work group comments on "Black Power, White Power, Shared Power":

"The majority of black people are not militant. Why don't whites see that when they step on blacks they are creating militant blacks?"

"If black power takes over, it will not stop when it becomes equal, but will continue."

"Whites are good, bad, industrious, lazy . . . what have you. Ditto for blacks. Can't we learn to work together like the separate fingers of a hand?"

Some work group comments on "Revolutionary Violence":

"Maybe white people have to learn to think black, but the art of being non-Establishment is more important. Revolution is basic. If the situation calls for violence, that's what you use. It is not important to be rational and explain yourself. An oppressed group tends to adopt the methods and weapons of those they oppose."

"The white community understands weapons as symbols of ultimate power. They don't understand the use of massive nonviolence. Therefore can we be expected to use it?"

"Violence ultimately means annihilation. We must use every other means available."

PART II

THE TECHNIQUES

3

Basic Principles of
Group Conversation

THE LEADERSHIP CHARACTERISTICS required for a Group Conversation are different from those required for a period of group discussion. The latter process consists mainly in the giving, getting and analyzing of facts about a problem, while Group Conversation is person-centered. Some people, because of training and experience, can, as the way opens, move into leading either of these group processes. Others may be more at home practicing one quality of leadership than the other.

When we say that Group Conversation is person-centered, that it takes the "host" or "hostess" type of mind, we refer to the ability to quickly relate people to each other and to make them feel at ease. But it is more than that. It takes a person who cares so much about others that he will not seek to dominate either consciously or unconsciously the spontaneous sharing of experiences that arises in true dialogue.* He will get his satisfaction from stimulating

* A further exposition of this principle will be found in *Learning to Work in Groups* by Matt Miles (New York, Bureau of Publications, Teachers College, Columbia University, 1959); *Group-Centered Leadership* by Thomas Gordon (Boston, Houghton Mifflin Co., 1955); and *The Miracle of Dialogue* by Reuel L. Howe (Greenwich, Conn., Seabury Press, 1953).

43

others into becoming more adequate participants in the group, and assisting in their personality development; he will feel secure enough in himself and in the group to be able to welcome spontaneity and not be upset if puzzling situations develop; he will discipline himself not to intellectualize during the Group Conversation nor to accept intellectualizing by others.

Leading Group Conversation is not a solo performance. Teamwork is necessary. There is need for more than one person in the planning; for it is a nurturing of the sharing of life experiences, the kind of give-and-take that hopefully will lead each member of the circle closer to achieving his personality potential. And there should *always* be a circle where all can see each other's faces.

The Social Psychology Involved

As seen by our example of Group Conversation in the meeting of union members, the leader holds in mind a few "pump-priming" or lead questions which he uses to structure the sharing. How he uses these with the co-operation of his co-leaders we shall show later. Here we offer a basic pattern for categories of lead questions which have been used with consistent success. They build on one another and can lead dramatically to a significant close:

—Memories that involve the senses—the feel, smells, tastes, sounds, colors
—Memories of activities we had with other children in home and at school, related to the topic
—Memories of what we did in our homes or schools, or in churches or synagogues

Memories connected with the senses are close to the threshold of consciousness, so these are drawn out first. From the sensory experiences, the next most natural area for easy sharing we have found to be about what we did with other children. Most participants recall with vivid excitement early play events in homes, neighborhoods or schools. The experiences we had with our families have deep meanings for us and sharing such memories builds toward a significant group feeling. The sharing of such tender material can lead individuals to a sense of renewal and to a mood of mutual acceptance and of rapport which could help them to work together.

Introducing the Idea

It is assumed that a group goal has been recognized and a fitting topic has been chosen. For example, in the case reported in Chapter 1 the goal was to help a Southern union develop mutual acceptance among its members. The topic, "Memories of Food for Breakfast," was chosen because the group had just had breakfast, while the lead questions fitted memories of people who grew up in the Bible belt of rural America.

At this point the leader will want to know how to introduce the idea of Group Conversation to new participants. This of course depends on the nature of the group and the reason for its coming together. If it is for a get-acquainted time, then the idea can be introduced simply as a time for matching memories. In a religiously motivated group, the reason given might be: "Since in a few moments we want to talk about some of our religious concerns, shall we start by sharing some of our earliest religious memories in the broadest sense of the term?"

One might quote Harry Overstreet, who, after participating in a Group Conversation, remarked: "Mature adults should come together more often for the sake of enjoying one another, and for the relaxation of doing things that have the life-sustaining seriousness of play." Our experience in leading hundreds of these Group Conversations is that, with few exceptions, persons are easily caught up in the mood of spontaneous give-and-take.

Assuming that a group of 20 to 40 people are in a circle in one's living room or church or union hall, and that two or three co-leaders have cooperated in thinking through something of what might take place, how does one start?

The leader may begin by assuring the group, if comprised mainly of strangers, that the purpose of the gathering is to become better acquainted and to relax and have a good time together. He may say something to this effect: "This is *not* a group discussion, such as we have when there is a problem to be considered, but Group Conversation, which is simply a way of matching our experiences around a topic of common interest. When one person is recounting his or her memories, the rest of us will find our own memories also bubbling over. I'll know by the expression on your face or the wave of your hand that you want to be the next to speak. Then, too, since singing together is relaxing, if anyone thinks of a song that matches a memory, mention it. If we know it, we'll sing; if not, we'll skip it. And lastly, since we want everyone to have the opportunity to talk, no one of us can talk too long."

Placing in Time and Locality

Help your participants recall where they were at eight or ten or twelve years of age. This is psychologically invaluable. It helps even the most shy to try his voice out before the group in a way that brings him a feeling of recognition and acceptance. It also helps the leader, who should make a special effort to remember what regions and countries are represented. Then, later, he can draw out certain memories from, let us say, France or California to round out the memory picture, or casually to invite the participation of the timid. This "placing" should come *after* the group has been given an explanation of a goal. They can then see the reason for it. The leader might proceed by saying, "First, we had better say who we are and where we were at the age of ten, twelve, or fourteen, since that is the age which will most easily bring out our similar memories."

"I was growing up in New York City." (The leader always goes first.) "Where were you? Let's go quickly around the circle telling where we were at that age. This will be the only time we shall go clockwise; after this, our sharing will be completely spontaneous." This last statement gives assurance to the reticent. In the placing, anyone may pass, but if another eagerly starts on memories, the leader can tactfully interrupt and say that memories will come later, and repeat his original statement that we are now only telling where we were at the age of ten or twelve or thereabouts. The leader may lighten the recital of place with a few brief remarks. Humor is to be encouraged.

The leader sits where he can see the faces of all the participants, and opposite his co-leader. If the group happens to be large—that is, 30 or more—he may find it natural to leave his chair occasionally, to move about in the center as he encourages people to take part. There is no need to be unduly concerned about a momentary feeling of unnaturalness at the start. This is usual with any meeting of strangers.

The placing done, the leader starts, in order to set the pattern so that others will know what is expected, with his own memories centered upon the sensory impressions evoked by the topic; but as soon as a face in the group lights up, he stops recounting his own memories and asks, "What is your memory?"

A co-leader may help, if no one else is yet ready, by quickly matching his memories with those of the leader. It sometimes takes a few moments for the process to get going. This part of the Group Conversation becomes a kind of "weaving" process, helped along, as the leader watches the faces, by such questions as these: "Is that like anything you did in your part of the country?" or, "Who has a similar memory, or even a contrasting one, for that, too, would be interesting?"

Weaving the Conversation

While a particular person is talking, the leader holds in mind a lead question which he thinks might come next. Often it comes from the group. Sorrowful remembrances are encouraged along with the pleasant memories. "Life ain't no bed of roses," to quote the poet, Langston Hughes. If, however, a bitter note is injected by some participant, it is received but the leader does not encourage more of the same. This group process is not therapy-centered, but as with any emotionally satisfying experience there is therapeutic value.

The Closing

The flow of the conversation must not stop abruptly just because the time is up. It is an experience that fits the mood. The leader watches his time and allows at least five or ten minutes for the closing. If he has asked for memories of what was done in church, temple or school, the symbolism of the season or the significance that has been voiced in some other topic, he picks up the serious note and suggests that the Group Conversation be brought to a close by looking at the deeper significance of the experience. He asks not that there be discussion, but that as a group there be thinking along such lines as these: "What did we have in our youth that the world needs today?" or, "Looking at the world as it is today, and thinking together as a group about our responsibility in meeting these needs, what do we as citizens in this community want to say to each other?" or "A few moments of silent thinking together might be good at this point." This period will not last long; short statements of conviction usually come from the group. Sometimes this is done with the group standing in a circle—if the leaders stand up with outstretched hands, most people will spontaneously stand and form a circle holding hands. Sometimes a song known to most picks up the mood, after which the serving of coffee is announced, and the participants begin to relate to each other on a one-to-one basis. And this, too, is valuable and necessary.

Group Movement and Contact

The physical contact of people in a group, as well as eye contact, can stimulate feelings of caring between persons. Holding hands in a circle is a fitting closing. A simple circle dance if it fits the mood, or moving as a group to the place for refreshments is psychologically valuable. Gordon Allport, of Harvard, stressed this after he participated in a Group Conversation: "Until we get this acceptance of others into our very muscles, glands and bones, we do not have it." The behavioral scientists are now also stressing this need.

At the beginning of our work we always planned for and used group movement, mainly around festivities connected with the change in the seasons. On such occasions participating in each other's folk dances was natural. Once a sensitive black school principal reported that when her anti-Negro Italian-American mothers were in the circle dance with her, she felt in her hands the moment when those two women accepted her. Today with the need to focus more on social action, we have used group movement less often, not because we feel it is less needed but because most of us have yet to learn how to do this with sensitivity and artistry. To see the importance of rhythmic body movements of a group, we have only to suggest here the image of twenty or thirty people, mixed in background, moving in a simple circle dance, forming a dome of hands, tips touching—hands of workers, hands of intellectuals; black, brown and white hands; old and young hands.

At such times Group Conversation approaches an art form. As defined by John Dewey in his *Art as Experience:* "Any experience is an art experience if it has harmony, balance and rhythm and if every successive part flows freely into what ensues, with no sacrifice of the self-identity of any of the parts. . . . Indeed, leaders often have the feeling that in the group process unrelated individuals like unrelated pigments become related in the art process."

It is best if group movement can be woven spontaneously, like songs, in the midst of the Group Conversation (as dancing "Here We Go, Looby Lu"), when someone relates a memory of the long-ago Saturday night bath. Sometimes a group, if the mood is right, can be directed by a group movement leader to the place where coffee is being served, and then released as a group. Sometimes, just before leaving for home, the participants form a circle to sing, with arms crossed, "Aloha" and "Auld Lang Syne" or "We Shall Overcome."

Importance of Memories and Feelings

There is a deep need today for emphasis on feelings because our scientific, analytical, objective culture has played up the intellect and played down the expression of feelings, so that many of us have lost our sense of wholeness and are cut off from our inner selves. Our psychologists are now beginning to draw our attention to the dangers of this imbalance.

But how can we get leaders and participants who are oriented toward social action to see the value of coming together to share their memories and feelings when they want to "get on with the job"? This usually means to them the giving of more facts about the problem, and the discussion of those facts and hopefully some united action. We, of course, see the need for facts and the logical use of those facts, but life has taught us that *most people do not act according to what they know, but according to what they feel about what they know.* There are many ways to appeal to people's emotions, but from long experience we have found that a period of Group Conversation which leads into discussion is an effective way to combine both approaches to human motivation, *i.e.* the emotional and the factual.

We do not ask the group's permission to share feelings, but as tactfully as possible we open up the process. Once they are in it, they find the renewal which comes from the "resurrection of the sense memories," to quote C. S. Lewis. It was this British writer who pleaded that we pay more attention to the intake of our senses "to make every pleasure into a channel of adoration . . . from the first taste of air when I go to the window . . . down to one's soft slippers at bedtime . . . these patches of godlight in the woods of our experience. . . . Don't talk to me of the illusions of memory: Why should what we see at the moment be more real than what we see from ten years distant?" *

Why Evoke Early Sensory Memories?

It is in our youth, especially the years of six to fourteen, after the first years of learning to fit into the culture of the family and society, and before the start of teenage stress, that the individual is most alert to the world about him. It is then that we explore the world with our senses—the sight, sound, smell, taste and feel of things and of people. It is then that we can run for the sheer joy of running and cry over the death of even a sparrow. These experiences and feelings become stored in the computers of our brain and are there as potential sources of energy and renewal. One year when our teams were being used by many PTA's in New York City, a former refugee from Hitler's Germany came often to the evening meetings, held in different parts of the city. Since he had no children in any of these schools, we asked him why he was interested in the PTA. His answer was, "It's not so much the PTA as myself. I grew up in Hamburg, Germany, and all the buildings in which I spent a happy childhood have been destroyed. When I can go back so often to those scenes in memory, I feel happier and more at home here in America."

It is the rare adult who cannot retrieve some pleasurable sense memory, no matter how deprived might have been his childhood. We have often noticed this with Negroes who grew up in the deep South's rural areas and feel "lost and lonely" in the big Northern city. With sensitivity they paint into the group's memory picture happy, sad, beautiful, humorous and bitter tones. It is all there, but only for the asking and accepting listener. So it is that by evoking early memories, and especially those connected with the senses, we put participants in contact with their sources of energy and renewal. For most of us city-bred intellectuals our sensory capacity

* *Letters to Malcolm—Chiefly on Prayer,* (New York, Harcourt, Brace & Co., 1962).

has become dulled. Dr. Herbert Otto writes of this: "We use our dulled senses to close ourselves off from both our physical and interpersonal environment. Today we also dull our perceptions of how other people feel." *

Another value gained from recalling these early memories is that it increases self-understanding and helps to overcome the modern problem of alienation. Matching memories (using "red letter days" as our topic) around events which stand out as having made us feel important—such as birthday parties, our first bicycle, winning school or athletic honors, confirmation services and their like—can help to reaffirm and reinforce a sense of identity; reviving such experiences reunites us with our roots. Extreme sensitivity to the kinds of memories which may come from participants needs to be practiced by the leader and co-leaders. They should welcome any memory which has in it the "red letter" feel for the individual, no matter how different, such as, "The day the whole gang praised the way I pitched a ball." On the other hand, the leader will allow the quiet one to sit there, relaxed, with no pressuring to participate vocally, drinking in and being renewed by the radiant happiness of others. He sees the joy on their faces, hears it in their voices, feels it, kinesthetically, in the touch of bodies in the close circle. (We advise a close circle and never sitting around a table.) Perhaps the silent participant did not have that joy as a child; but if his bitterness has not completely cut him off from others, he senses and shares some of that happiness now. This is what is meant by the psychic unity of humanity, by "no man is an island." Is this transcendent feeling-need related to our modern problem of alienation? Is enough attention being given to this need? We who lead Group Conversations know this "drinking in of joy" has happened, sometimes because the quiet ones tell us how they feel after the experience. They try to put into words why they did not participate. Perhaps it was that "I grew up in an orphan asylum," or "My father was a terrible drunkard."

Sometimes the participant is already so emotionally mature that he has "accepted" his deprived background and can tell the group

* Dr. Herbert A. Otto, "New Light on the Human Potential," *Saturday Review,* 12/2/69. Dr. Otto is chairman of the National Center for the Exploration of Human Potential. For the importance of paying more attention to our senses, see also *Sense Relaxation, Below Your Mind,* Gunther & Fusco (New York, Collier, 1969).

of his father's excessive drinking and of his own childhood anguish. This sharing helps lead the inarticulate participant to a healthy acceptance of his own disturbing childhood experiences. Even though these unpleasant memories may not be vocalized in the group, the very act of listening to others, inwardly comparing one's self with these others, helps the listener to take a step toward emotional maturity.

It is well to emphasize that in Group Conversation *one is never pressed to share*. The placing question is the only one that asks each participant to give his name and to say where he grew up. The leader watches faces, and if he notices a conflicting expression asks: "Would you like to pass?" One man who often participated in Group Conversation, and hence must have found some satisfaction in it, could never go beyond "I grew up on a farm in Maine." Later in privacy he gave the reason: "My father was a terrible drunkard."

We see then that this sharing of childhood experiences helps us in understanding others. After one such experience in a church group one of the participants said of another: "After hearing just that little bit of Mary's childhood I will never again feel irritated with her." But these values are not deliberately elicited from a group which is moving towards some social action. Perhaps the person himself is not conscious of why he feels better, younger, more in touch with others. It is well that the leaders do take the time to insure this kind of sharing, whether of anguish or of rejoicing, which can bring us close to one another.

And we might add that the success we have had in the sharing of early memories is based not only on the fact that with few exceptions adults love to talk about their youth, but also on their being removed sufficiently from it to speak freely if the social situation encourages it. We do not feel responsible for our youth, whether our experience be good or bad, pleasant or unpleasant.

The Team Is Important

We need to emphasize the importance of team leadership. Even if a leader is invited to some group at a distance, he should arrive the day before, get briefing on the group and in that briefing ask one or two to help in co-leading. Today, in many kinds of group activities sophisticated adults often feel they are being manipulated. Aside from the need of a leader to maintain a non-dogmatic manner, it helps if the leadership is spread out. Then, too, there are various co-leadership duties in assisting the leader. What this consists of will become evident as we proceed. Since the goal of many groups is to proceed into a discussion of their problem or social issue, one co-leader should be proficient in and ready for leading the discussion period. Group discussion is quite different from Group Conversation, for the various facts related to a problem must be analyzed in group discussion. Group Conversation, as we have said, is a pulling together and a relating of parts to a whole. Like an artist who reaches into his palette for colors which he puts together artistically, a Group Conversation leader feelingly relates to one another the original mere collection of individuals. It is for this reason that it is often difficult for the same individual to move quickly from leading one type of thinking to another.

Utilizing Specialists

Sometimes instead of discussion the group need is to hear from a specialist certain facts related to its interest. Specialists in early childhood education, credit unions, open housing, community mental hygiene are among those who have been used in our Group Conversations. When this is the case, the specialist participates in the early memory sharing. A co-leader then will introduce the specialist and act as chairman or moderator for the remainder of the meeting.

An example of the use of a specialist in a Group Conversation took place in a small county in Georgia. In the changeover from dispensing surplus government food to giving food stamps, the Office of Economic Opportunity funded teaching of 400 rural families on relief to select their food according to the best nutritional standards by using a form of Group Conversation during which the recipients in small groups, remembering with nostalgic overtones foods of their youth, became motivated not only to listen, but also to act on the advice of the nutritionist. The specialist, in learning to use the group method, was able then to teach other basic facts such as the close relationship between good food habits of pregnant women and baby foods to the development of the child's I.Q.*

* See the report in Chapter 7 of the Food Stamp and Nutrition Project and the report in Chapter 6.

Songs in Group Conversation

One role for a co-leader is that of song leader. Songs help greatly if the aim of the group's meeting is to become acquainted, or to have a relaxed, entertaining yet meaningful time together. Then the topic chosen may be related to the change of the seasons or the celebration of some event—the birth of a baby among the members, a confirmation, or the observance of a retirement. In this kind of experience it helps to have the group sing together. But sometimes even in the midst of serious sharing on a deep psychological or spiritual level a well-chosen song may be just the experience needed.

The song leader is one familiar with the songs known by most in the group. Song books or sheets should never be passed out. To do so destroys the developing mood. One line and the chorus are enough, and sometimes only the chorus. In this kind of situation it is not the perfection of the singing, but the singing together, even if falteringly, by most members of the group which matters. Of course the more perfect the singing, the greater the aesthetic value, and the more easily the group comes to feel its unity. Spontaneity is stressed here also, for the songs should evolve out of what is being said in the group.

Today's songs popular with youth in the folk style of our time are often related to our social problems, and not only to joy and longing, but also to hunger, struggle, pain, and to our search for peace. Among other songs of social significance, Bob Dylan's "Blowin' in the Wind" is well enough known for its use in Group Conversation when it fits. One might add Josh White's "One Meat Ball" as a poignant expression of hunger in our affluent society.

The spirituals are especially valuable and easy for group singing. These songs and the blues * arose from and still express a group's struggle for freedom and should be sung by all of us who are concerned about that freedom: "I'm So Glad Trouble Don't Last Always," "Listen to the Lambs," "Walk Together, Children," to mention a few. For the song leader to "line out" the words of the next line of the song is an easy way to help all participate.

* For an inspiring statement of the origin and role of the blues songs in American life, see "The Gift of Blackness" by Vincent Harding in the summer 1967 issue of *Katalligete,* published by the Committee of Southern Churchmen, 1207 Eighteenth Avenue South, Nashville, Tenn. 37212.

The freedom songs which kept up the spirits of the marchers both in and out of jail during the height of the civil rights struggle in the 1960's should also be used when they fit into the present struggle: "Ain't Gonna Let Nobody Turn Me Around," "Freedom Now," Woody Guthrie's "This Land Is Your Land," and many others. "We Shall Overcome" of course has brought tears, courage and a sense of conviction to millions of Americans.

When the Group Is Large

Group Conversation is best for groups of 20 to 40, but sometimes, as in a Parents Association meeting, there may be need to accommodate from 300 to 400. We do not advise starting with such a number, but after some experience we find that it is possible to allow for some spontaneity in a large group and still handle the situation. First, there should be a planning session of 15 to 20 persons who will represent the groups expected at the meeting, and who will act as co-leaders, scattered through the audience. A sample of memories will be matched, and songs and games recalled, during the planning session where the topic will be given a dry run. With such a large group it is best to seat them in concentric circles small enough so that participants can hear one another. The leader needs to be on his feet in the center throughout most of the session. He will find his own way to take away the formality of the meeting. If he has a feel for the theater, it helps. For placing the people, he may ask for a show of hands of those who grew up in New England, the far West, the deep South, then come back to the natives of the local community. "And if we are really lucky, we shall have people who grew up in other countries." Almost every American audience will have some persons of other nationalities.

In a large group, it is necessary to be certain that the suggested songs and dances are done well. A good pianist and song leader are invaluable and should function as co-leaders. If possible, secure the services of a professional folk singer and a folk dancer. These "stars" must, of course, weave their performances into the conversation in as spontaneous a way as possible. Acknowledgment or identification of these performers comes best at the end of the session.

For the ending, opportunity can be given for short expressions of conviction related to the topic. A community leader who has prestige for the group may be invited to sum up the comments and contributions of the meeting. Or the session may end simply with one or two appropriate songs, a jolly folk song and a large circle dance at the last. It may also, particularly with professional artists, be brought to a more elaborate finale.

Social Education Through Happy Memories *

For the large group situation we offer one report:

> The meeting was one of about 100 women, most of them middle-aged, who with few exceptions were officers of small, local organizations. The leader arranged them in two circles of seats, with space enough in the middle for an occasional demonstration of a game or a dance, and a piano at one side.
>
> The chosen theme of the conversation was "Spring is in the air." The setting was arranged to suggest that "we are twelve years old, in the home of our childhood; it is the first day of spring," and in drawing from it a mounting sense of participation in a universal drama. . . .
>
> From the very start women who, to judge from the way in which they first exchanged whispered remarks with their neighbors, and then spoke in a very low voice, were unaccustomed to speak in a gathering of this size, smilingly recalled childhood scenes.
>
> They spoke of the smell of the soil on the first warm day of the year; the first flowers in the grass; the foods and cakes prepared and eaten on spring holidays; the "Fasching" which, though it also has another significance, was a boisterous welcoming of spring. They spoke of the new clothes; the outdoor games played at this time of year; the cozy fire enjoyed while the nights were yet cold; the family seated near the iron stove, the tiled oven, or the open hearth; the children's Saturday night bath in front of the fire; the stories told by a grandmother; the reading aloud, and the family prayers.
>
> Every once in a while such reminiscences were punctuated with a song or a dance game, and usually they were known

* From *Adult Leadership,* March 1958. The author, Bruno Lasker, a leader in adult education, was for many years associate editor of *Survey Magazine.* (Quoted by permission.)

by enough of the members who joined in, even though they had learned it in this country from a Russian-born mother or a Danish grandfather.

As soon as the proceedings started, I noticed that eyes lighted up and that what was said called up pleasant associations in every mind. People who an hour earlier might have said, "I dislike Negroes," or "I'm not in the least interested in Estonia," listened because what was said reminded them of their own childhood. . . .

There was no hurrying from point to point, and no attempt to force upon the group anything that was not ready to spring from the memory of a member. Everything was—or at least seemed—spontaneous.

The proceedings were kept under control, yet the speed was noticeably growing; little points cumulatively led to larger and more significant points. And the conversation, in spite of its intimate and personal character, led to a climax: on this occasion a unanimous joining in the singing of a Negro spiritual begun by a member of the group and, following it, of "America, the Beautiful."

In short, under skillful conductorship, the "conversation" became a sort of symphony. There was a definite beginning and a definite end; a major theme ran through it, varied and accompanied by minor themes. Each "section," here no strings and brass and concussion instruments, but the native American elements—composed of many different races and cultures—made a harmonious pattern. In this heterogeneous group, evolved out of the diverse strands, the experience will linger long in the mind after the meeting is over. After such an experience, need people wonder just what it is that makes a united America?

4

Preparation and Follow-up

IT IS, AS WE HAVE SAID, imperative that you do not work alone, but that you share at the beginning your responsibility with two or three others. Knowing the group you are to lead, its auspices and what its areas of interest and goals are, will enable you to choose a fitting topic for the memory theme. In this preparation session, your team will draw on its own memories related to the topic. You may want to try more than one topic before finalizing it. Rough notes are taken, so the leader can later work out in his own mind a series of lead questions based on the thinking of the team. These he shares with his co-leaders before the session.

Choosing and Developing a Topic

In previous reports we have explained in detail how we have used topics around the seasonal festivals for developing mutual acceptance among America's many ethnic groups. Recently such a sophisticated modern as Harvey Cox, the author of *The Secular City,* reminds us of the psychological and spiritual value of festivals:

> While gaining the whole world, western man has been losing his own soul. He has purchased prosperity at the cost of a staggering impoverishment of the vital elements of life. These

58

elements are festivity—the capacity for genuine revelry and joyous celebration and fantasy—the faculty for envisioning radically alternative life situations . . . They enable man to relate himself to the past and to the future . . . The festival, the special time when ordinary chores are set aside while man celebrates some event, affirms the sheer goodness of what is, or observes the memory of a god or hero . . . Festivity is more closely related to memory, and fantasy is more akin to hope.*

In this manual, however, we give attention to the development of topics closely related to the need for reducing social tensions—they can be used with people of varying age, educational, professional or economic experiences. We have evoked their remembrances mainly around such topics as: Work, Food, Sense of Time, School Days, Red-Letter Days, Storms, Life as a Journey, Communication, Books I have Loved, Our Most Creative Moment, Simplicity Today, and Growth—to mention only a few.

Care should be taken not to choose too small a section of a subject for a topic. For example, instead of Trees, more can be developed out of On Being Close to Nature. This topic could lead into a fruitful discussion on conservation.

The team, as we have said, meets first not only to select a topic (any which they feel will fit the goals of the group), but to develop it. To do this after choosing a topic, the team members hold in mind the sequence of memories from their personal sensory experiences to their shared experiences with others, and then an ending.

The major step in developing a Group Conversation topic which will relate the feelings of the participants to some phase or phases of the issue and then lead into fruitful discussion, is to visualize the group which is to participate. We will say it is mainly middle-class and middle-aged—an adult religious group or a suburban women's club. Then one should engage them in an imaginary dialogue about the issue. If it is the guaranteed annual income, one might ask about their attitudes on present-day welfare; if it is on busing children to attain integrated schools, then one visualizes their attitudes toward that issue. Then the leader and co-leaders share their own early memories around experiences which in the pending group situation might set the emotional tone for an open-minded discussion of the problem.

* Cox, Harvey, *Festival of Fools* (New York, Harper & Row, 1969).

We present here as adaptable examples a few topics which have been developed and used successfully by our team. We will leave the introductory part of these topics to the particular needs of each situation, presenting here some typical lead questions. Leaders, of course, are admonished to select the questions which will most likely fit their own experiences *and* the memories of the participants whom they expect to be present. From this, the necessity to study local customs and aspirations becomes obvious. Begin where people are.

A Sampling of Topics

Life as a Journey. This is a valuable topic for youth or adults, or both together.

INTRODUCTION: The placing can be, along with their names, a two-sentence description of the place in which the participants grew up—farm, small town, or city.

LEAD QUESTIONS: What is our earliest recollection of a road or a street? What time of year is it, and do we see anything moving? What early journey with our family comes back to us? Is it the journey or the arrival that comes back to us more vividly? What was our first trip alone? Did any of us ever run away from home or plan to do so? What trip became the most significant in that it deeply influenced our lives?

ENDING: This will depend on the nature and goal of the group. Religious groups will move naturally into symbols and meanings significant for them. The biblical story of man's journey from the Garden of Eden on can become a symbol of the journey of each human being.*

One emphasis on which Americans in general might end such a topic is the idea that we all have pioneer blood in our veins. In this space age, what are some of the new dimensions in individual, family, and community life that we should be mapping out as modern pioneer? If desired this could serve as a transition into a discussion of social problems which concern them. As an example, there is the

---

* In many churches the Group Conversation method has been used effectively for the regular mid-week meeting. The leaders choose the topic to fit group needs and give the pertinent reading of Bible and vocal prayer at the end instead of at the start of the service. A co-leader familiar with the Bible can choose verses according to what comes up in Group Conversation.

need for a clearer understanding of the guaranteed annual income to solve the problem of welfare.

Work . . . Income . . . Poverty. To relate the question of guaranteed annual income to the topic of work, some lead questions might be: In our growing-up home, was there an attitude of work for work's sake? Specifically how has technology changed attitudes toward work—dishwashing, for instance? Did our experiences as children give us a sense of the joy of work? Have any of us been in any kind of a crisis—illness or sudden loss of family income—when we had to receive help from outside the family? How did we feel?

If no one in the pending group is likely to have had experiences of being on welfare, then the leaders ask themselves if it is possible to invite two or three people who have had such an experience. If this is impossible, then it is valuable for the leaders to read a brief description of welfare experiences as from Dick Gregory's *Nigger.* In this he tells how he felt as a child when his family was on welfare. The sociological analysis by Kenneth Clark in *Dark Ghetto* * will also be valuable in the leaders' preparation. The open mind of the leader is basic to a free-flowing group discussion. They may want to share this statement with the group to stimulate reactions:

> The overwhelming majority of the poor don't want to be poor. They have been kept in poverty, in some cases for two or more generations. They are the victims of technological changes, of wrong-headed economic policies, of political powerlessness, of discrimination, of the environment of poverty itself. Their despair and demoralization can be dispelled only by the opening of genuine economic opportunity. When such opportunity is provided, along the lines suggested in the "Freedom Budget," the cycle of poverty can and will be broken.**

For such a complex problem as the guaranteed annual income, leaders will probably want to invite a specialist who will lead the discussion. This person will share his early experiences with the group. The leaders will, of course, prepare themselves for leading

* See also, *Manchild in the Promised Land* by Claude Brown (New York, Macmillan, 1965)—a vivid first-person account of growing up in Harlem.
** See *A "Freedom Budget" for All Americans* by the A. Philip Randolph Institute, 217 Park Avenue South, New York City, 10010.

up to the problem by carefully studying the pros and cons of the issue and will introduce the moderator.

School Desegregation. If school desegregation is chosen, then a similar procedure is followed: What are probable attitudes of participants in the group one is to lead, and what might be some early experiences related to the subject? In their preparation session the leaders evoke their own early school experiences.

LEAD QUESTIONS could include some of the following: The kind of school or schools one attended—was it segregated? well- or ill-provided with up-to-date teaching materials? crowded or small classes? Was there a lack of healthy competition? How did one get to school? Did street gang battles occur? How did one feel when his family moved into a new neighborhood? How was one treated by a prejudiced teacher as compared with that of a teacher "who saw my potential"?

Time. There are many deeply meaningful memories as well as entertaining experiences which may be developed around the topic of "Time," in any kind of group at any time of the year. Of course, it fits especially at the New Year season. Sophisticated participants will share deep philosophical ideas, and youth groups will receive stimulation for thinking out their own philosophy, especially if a few "wise" adults are present. It is particularly enriching if two or three Oriental or South American or African guests are present, for they may be from cultures with a sense of time different from ours.

INTRODUCTION AND PLACING: After a fitting brief introduction the placing might be: What was our earliest feeling about time? May we go around the circle telling where we were from the ages of eight to twelve, and describing in no more than two or three sentences the memory of a clock that comes back to us? The song "My Grandfather's Clock" usually evokes many a picture of a clock on the stairs.

LEAD QUESTIONS: How did we first learn to tell time? What kind of person taught us? Did we have a sense of mystery in connection with the concept of time? of the seasons? of space? What jingles did we learn, like "Thirty days hath September"? What childhood verses, like "In the winter I get up at night/ And dress by yellow candlelight./ In summer quite the other way/ I have to go to bed by day."

What celebrations or events marked the pasage of time? of night and day? of summer and winter? birthdays? New Year's Day? other seasonal events? (Not all these need to be used in one session.)

What is psychological time? When is time short, and when is it long? How is time experienced by the very young, and by the very old?

ENDING: The possible endings will be as varied as the interests and needs of the participants. What is the meaning of "I do not have time" in our age of time-saving devices? If anyone is present from a culture which does not have our feeling about the importance of many activities, and of being on time at each of them, it would be good to compare these values. Here can be seen values in cultural diversity.

Two Sample Group Conversation Reports

TOPIC: The Quaker testimony, "Do you keep to simplicity and moderation in your speech, your manner of living, and your pursuit of business?"

INTRODUCTION: This will depend on the make-up of the group. Are they Quakers checking their lives against one of their testimonies, or a group of young people asking themselves how they can live a relevant life in today's fast-changing world?

PLACING: Where we grew up, and the nature of our father's work.

LEAD QUESTIONS (not all need to be used in a single session):

What family or families in our community did we consider rich when we were little? Do we have any memory of feeling poorer than others? What incident stands out when we got a new dress or suit? Do we have a lingering sense of rivalry with our peers about clothes? Were we ever punished for using "bad language"? What was our idea of success as teenagers? Did any of our families interpret Christian humility in a way which might have hindered our development? What is simplicity to us today? Someone has said, "It's the absence of all that's not necessary." What rivalry are we caught up in today? Possessions, professions, opinions? What is the good life for us? Does it include beauty, creativity, fellowship, spiritual growth? What is a good standard of living? More and more things to consume or better things to appreciate? Movies? TV? Does the sense of rivalry, despair, even fear around us affect our being able to lead a life of simplicity? How can we help each other?

To the leader: You will sense if the following should be presented to your group:

Do we tend to regard our personal feelings, sensations, intuitions and even our instincts as inferior and contemptible? Someone has said that modern man must learn to appreciate the importance of happiness of his inner world, that our creative powers come from the realm of the irrational, that the intellect can only select. When have we, recently, expressed some of our inner feelings as in spontaneously dancing or singing to music, even alone? In this sense is it important to fantasize? to laugh? to loaf? Can members of a small understanding group help each other toward this kind of release? Or is it something we can only do for ourselves? Is any of this relevant to the life of simplicity?

CLOSING: This will develop out of the group experience.

TOPIC: Communication (for teenagers).

INTRODUCTION: Reference might be made to the complexity of the physical communication of the astronauts while orbiting. This Group Conversation is about communication of the heart—do we really understand one another? Yet we have always communicated in some way even from babyhood.

PLACING: How many individuals do we have now at home with whom we must communicate?

LEAD QUESTIONS: Do we recall feeling close to a doll or a teddy-bear which we took to bed with us as a child? What pet was close to us? Dog? Cat? Bird? Who remembers a very close first friendship outside the family?

The group may share how these levels of communication differ, leading perhaps to the responsibility of each individual to find *Who am I?* and ways of expressing his uniqueness in communication. This quote could be used: "There is no one in the world like you and never was and never will be; it is your excuse for being." It will be valuable if the leader can share his experience of a failure at communication. As an example, one friend at college was so eager for acceptance that she allowed others to think of her as different from what she really was. What's wrong with this?

How can we begin to find "Who and what I am"? Going in for

sports? art? music? Would the keeping of a diary help? What would
it contain?

Someone has said that "the measure of a man is the size of the
thing it takes to get his goat." Can we recall instances or situations
or people who push us to express anger? Have any of us participated in an encounter group when the expression of one's anger is
encouraged? How does one feel? Compare with the opposite feeling
—closeness to another. Are such experiences helpful in knowing
who we are? Can we recall a moment when we felt very close, below the verbal level, to another person? Is this confined to those on
our own age level? Has any individual helped us find ourselves—
what teacher or older person inspired us? Does the generation gap
today prevent this? How do the pressures of conformity keep us
from knowing ourselves?

CLOSING will develop out of the content in the sharing.

A Checklist for Leading

To expedite the preparation time of the leader and co-leaders,
we suggest use of this checklist:

INTRODUCTION. After welcoming and stating why the group has
gathered, state the difference between Group Conversation and
group discussion. Be informal. Make others feel at ease.

PLACING. Say, "We will go around only once clockwise." Leader
goes first.

LEAD QUESTIONS. According to the nature of the topic, individual memories around senses, activities with other children, fun,
games, etc. What was done in homes, churches, synagogues or
schools? Again the leader shares first in order to give a model of
what is expected.

CLOSING. Something significant. Try to recognize in the spontaneity of the conversation a natural bridge to the ending. If discussion is the need, try to move into it naturally, or if the subject
for a discussion has been announced for "after coffee," relate the
ending in some way to that subject.

WEAVING. When possible, pick up thread of next category from
something said in the group. Trust the group. Seek spontaneity.
Don't spend too much too much time on any one category; not all
participants have to respond to each lead question.

CO-LEADER'S ROLE. Develop topic with leader; observe faces of participants; help bring in the latecomer and the shy; help deflect the too-long talker; introduce songs or group movement if appropriate; help with closing.

Words of Caution

This running description of how a Group Conversation grows from start to finish needs to be followed by a few important warnings that the leader should bear in mind. Beware of:
—the too-long talker;
—a leaderless, willy-nilly conversation;
—imposing a feeling of pressure to participate;
—any spirit of competition or controversy;
—encouraging the further expression of a bitter note;
—poor timing by dwelling too long on any one category;
—loss of group attention, by being interrupted by latecomers;
—using any songs, statements, or terms not fully acceptable to all members of the group present—for example, telling any jokes at the expense of anyone else (we must remember that laughing *with* others unites, but laughing *at* others separates);
—tendency to polarize Americans into two groups—though sometimes it will be necessary to begin with separate groupings, our aims should be to mix all groups in dialogue.

An additional word of caution is necessary about the use of terms, for it is easy for the novice to use a wrong one. Use words or phrases that give feelings of being included rather than excluded. Thus we say "those of us of Negro background" * or "those of us of Jewish or Christian faith." Never should a leader say "you Jews" or "you Christians" or "you Negroes," or even "you people."

Do not expect all members of particular groups to be talented in the same way. Not all Afro-Americans are able to dance or to sing well. There is a great variety of talent in every group. A few blacks are still sensitive about spirituals, though these songs are recognized the world over as great art. There seems to be a spiritual to fit almost every need, and the right one often comes up to charge a group with a deep, meaningful feeling. But other people also know

---

* These terms may change from time to time. Today the use of the word "black" is preferred by a growing number of Afro-Americans.

these songs; and so we need not look only to Negro participants to lead the group in singing them.

Follow-up of Group Conversation Sessions

The teamwork of leader and co-leaders should extend beyond the planning and conducting of the actual Group Conversation. They may wish to come together almost immediately afterward to evaluate the experience. They will want to share with one another what they feel to have been the high points of the Group Conversation and to determine in what ways they fell short of accomplishing their aims. Did they allow for enough spontaneity? Were the over-all goals (release of tension, more meaningful communication) accomplished to any degree? Although the leaders have had in this Group Conversation a common experience, each has seen the group process from a different angle. The interchange will be helpful in later experiences of this kind.

The nature of the follow-up will depend on the auspices under which the Group Conversation is held. If a particular institution sponsors it, such as neighborhood gatherings, clubs, community centers, various organizations or some kinds of government agencies, then the session's follow-up can be a part of the regular responsibilities of the teacher or leader of such a group. In fact, it is quite likely that the leader's or teacher's regular duties will be made easier, for interest is quickened, certain intergroup problems may begin to diminish, and creativity is released with the increased spirit of goodwill. But in any case it is valuable to sustain groups after they start to evolve by giving effective follow-up in leadership guidance and materials.

Some leaders have developed a series of related topics, so planned from the start for a specific goal as to find volunteers for social action in the community. Others, at the end of the first session, have simply asked: "Who wants to explore this subject further with us?" Of course, they are ready with suggestions for the group to act on. Thus it is that leaders will realize that the use of Group Conversation is one of the increasing number of small–group tools being used today to help individuals overcome their own tensions and to communicate with others so they can work together more effectively to overcome the injustices. Then "haters will no longer be making haters out of their victims."

Outline for Report, Evaluation and Follow-up

> PLACE
> AUSPICES
> CATEGORY(IES) OF PARTICIPANTS
> NUMBER OF PARTICIPANTS
> LEADER AND CO-LEADER(S)
> GOAL
> TOPIC
> INTRODUCTION
> PLACING
> LEAD QUESTIONS
> CLOSING
> EVALUATION BY LEADER AND CO-LEADER(S)
> FOLLOW-UP PLANS (drawn from participants' suggestions
>   and remarks, and from evaluation above)

A Typical Training Workshop

After a Group Conversation team has gained sufficient experience in leading, it should set up its own training workshop to assist others in learning how to apply the techniques. This can become a small-group, do-it-yourself movement in a community, and can spread, like strawberry plants, by sending out shoots.

The following is a format for training workshops which we have used most often. Three sessions are planned to provide experiential knowledge of the method; it is more effective if the sessions can be in fairly close sequence, such as on three successive evenings or, at most, three successive weeks.

SESSION ONE: *The initial demonstration,* followed by reactions of participants to the experience and brief discussion as to the use of this method in community activities. Up to 25 could take part in this, but the training part of the workshop, the next two sessions, should have not more than 16-18 trainees.

SESSION TWO: *A second demonstration* of a half-hour duration, with another topic and another leader team, adhering closely to the structuring of Group Conversation, and followed by an analysis of the structuring of Group Conversation. See Chapter 3 for the six points of structure: introduction, placement, lead questions (categories), the art of weaving, closing, and the co-leader's role.

The trainees, now divided into teams of two—a leader and a co-leader—choose and develop a topic. Often this is done while sharing a simple lunch.

Practice sessions. Each team is given thirty minutes, followed by a ten-minute critique by a person trained or experienced in the use of the method. To insure practice time the participants may be divided into two circle groups. To provide variety, each team of two joins the other circle after finishing its session.

Repetition of the process allows the participant to listen with the idea of evaluating how the leadership promotes the flow of interaction and with the intention of applying the critique of the experience (the analysis) to developing his own leadership patterns.

Secondary gains may be the delight of getting to know other individuals better, and understanding better what some of his own experiences have meant in his personality development.

SESSION THREE. The practice of the leader and co-leader role continues until each trainee has experiential knowledge of the Group Conversation process. This is an application session on ways to help trainees see how they can use Group Conversation effectively in their own organizations or community groups.

Back home, trainees are encouraged to reinforce their newfound skill in a "second-level leading" as a practice step beyond the initial training. If there is no natural opportunity, such as a meeting of a committee or group, friends may be invited for an evening of fun and communication in which Group Conversation techniques are used.

Training Workshops in Ten Cities

SITUATION: At the invitation of Dr. Martin Luther King, Jr., we instituted within the SCLC (Southern Christian Leadership Conference) a Dialogue Department to "provide the power of dialogue when heart can reach out to heart in the search for truth, in the spirit of reconciliation." We set up first in Atlanta and then in nine other Southern and Northern cities,* dialogue workshops as a

* Atlanta, Ga.; Louisville, Ky.; St. Louis, Mo.; Nashville, Tenn.; Columbus and Westerville, O.; Richmond, Ind.; New York, N.Y.; Washington, D.C., and Birmingham, Ala.

training program for lay and professional leaders. Always the workshops were integrated. A pattern established in these cities follows.

Each trainee after his practice session in the workshop used his own home or that of his co-leader (usually a member of the opposite race) for further practice leading. To this the co-leaders invited their own friends and neighbors. A critique of the leading of these further practice sessions was done in a midweek meeting. The next step was to offer one's services to a community organization such as the local PTA, church or community action group, informal or officially sponsored.

FOLLOW-UP: Soon after we began our training in Atlanta, the War on Poverty started, with the Office of Economic Opportunity reaching to the local level of the cities in which we worked. Because these OEO programs welcomed the volunteer leadership of our trainees, our follow-up related closely to that agency's program in each city. Hence the topics chosen were more related to community needs, as "Early Experiences with Money" if the community meeting was to focus on credit unions; if the community meeting was focused on how to get the best results from government surplus foods, then the topic might be "My First Successful Cooking." In some of the cities it was possible to train a selected group of leaders on how to set up training workshops to "develop and train others in an endless chain," to use Dr. King's word.

SECOND-LEVEL PRACTICE SESSIONS IN ONE CITY. Because of the fact that our program of training in each of the ten cities was similar, we are using here only a report from one city (St. Louis, Mo.), showing how trainees started to use their newly-learned group skill. This report shows not only the various goals, but under what community auspices and goals the method can be adapted and used. Our ten second-level practice sessions, involving 16 trainees as leaders or co-leaders, were held from Tuesday to Friday following the first training weekend. The visiting trainer attended all but one as a resource observer in order to be able to evaluate the leadership and to discuss it at the second weekend meeting of the trainees, when a self-understanding session would be held. Eight of these were in various Gateway Center Stations; two were in homes. One hundred and seventy-two new people participated. Some were Human Development Corporation staff; some, local residents; and about 12 were from the Friends Meeting, one of the sponsoring groups.

In order to help a group of women decide how to go about getting more recreational facilities for their community, as well as to give participants some insight in working with school dropouts, the volunteer leaders chose for their memory-evoking topic, "School Days and Games."

To motivate young people, the team (two teachers) took for its topic our own growing-up period—physical, mental and spiritual growth and showing what had motivated us.

A small group of neighbors in a home found that sharing their memories of spring was not only relaxing, but enabled them to know each other better.

At another center, where a specialist in consumer education was scheduled to talk to a group of women on how to get the most by way of nutrition and taste out of the government surplus food commodities, the leader first led the Group Conversation around memories of foods and family activities at the dining table.

One evening a gathering of 30 people, very mixed as to race and religion, was divided into two groups with different topics. One started with memories about *work,* and the other, *growth.* At the end of the evening the two groups met together to share and to evaluate their experience. There was much enthusiasm for fostering this type of meeting which gives people of various backgrounds living in a community a feeling of commonality.

At the Human Development Corporation headquarters with 19 members of the field staff, the leaders used *communication* as the topic. Memories of feeling close to pets and peers were contrasted with feelings of lonelines because of real or imagined inferiority.

In two groups led by pastors, the topic of *spring* was effectively used by one of the trainees who works with students from abroad. This experience showed the need for incorporating into our local groups these young people who are in our nearby universities. Americans need their broadening influence, and they need to know more facts of American life than simply the academic. Together there would come the feeling of international unity so needed today.

One of the pastors reported his work with "a summer camp staff":

A summer camp staff for the Missouri Conference Youth Ministry Workshop shared in a conversation on streets and directions, drawing us all much closer together as persons.

These same staff members led similar conversations at the start of the weeklong workshop itself, which did a great deal to set a tone of openness and sharing for the whole camp.

I held one semi-conversation with first- and second-graders about pets. It was the best talk I had ever had with them. A similar topic formed the subject of our conversation with a group of young people around a picnic table at the zoo.

OTHER CITIES. The New York group, like the Atlanta group, formed its own organization, became incorporated and gathered some funds for its activities. One became the New York Friends Center Workshop, Inc.* and the other the Atlanta Dialogue Center, Inc.** Both these groups have concentrated on offering monthly training workshops, followed by bi-weekly practice and guidance sessions in Group Conversation. In New York, a steering committee offered teams to lead Group Conversation in homes and community organizations.

The Louisville, Ky., group, after several training sessions had a group of trainees who volunteered their time to co-lead groups on the local level. They cooperated with specialists in credit unions, consumer education and mental hygiene. One community council in a Louisville suburb used the method for six months to create a greater feeling of unity within the Newburg neighborhood (about 1500 families). A letter from the Council President says:

> After our regular and intensive use of Group Conversation for six months, we then developed a system of Resident Contacts who contact the residents on their block once a month to advise them of Council activities, and to take their problems to the Council. The Resident Contacts meet with one another once a month and use a modified version of Group Conversation.

A letter from the Executive Director of the Louisville Mayor's Commission on Human Rights contained this paragraph:

> Although the value of this program, at this time, can only be measured in terms of its meaning to the participants, there is so much evidence of this, that I am confident that application of the Dialogue Method in the poverty areas, will prove

* 15 Rutherford Place, New York, N. Y., 10003.
** 110 Blackland Drive, N.W., Atlanta, Ga., 30305.

to be of inestimable value in releasing the considerable potential of the poor. Their need to be effectively articulate in order to truly become a part of the main stream of the life in this community, is of utmost importance.

ONGOING RESULTS. With the Dialogue Department of the SCLC having to be closed for lack of funds and hence there being no central office on a national level, we have no assurance that most of the local groups have gone on training others. However, the members of the Atlanta Dialogue Center, Inc., have conducted about ten more Training Workshops as well as being involved as individuals in Economic Opportunity, Atlanta, schools, etc. on a volunteer basis; and the New York Friends Center Workshop, Inc., has continued sponsoring workshops regularly, giving about eight a year for three years. We do know that for the most part, people of the sort who took the training are so involved in jobs and other regular organizations that they literally could not afford the time to keep another organization going. Many of them feel that Group Conversation has become their most valuable tool for moving the groups with which they work quickly into whatever project is at hand.

It has been pointed out to us that a cardinal value, even if there had been no other value, in most of the Southern cities is that this training experience and its follow-up afforded for many their only opportunity for interracial socializing. The need for this kind of socializing increases every day.

PART III

APPLICATIONS

5

Reducing Group Tensions

GROUP CONVERSATION has been founded on the concept that a healthy self-acceptance precedes the acceptance of others. It was a ten-year-old Chinese-American lad who put this truth in a positive way when he said to his classmates, "We Chinese shake hands with ourselves, because if you are a friend of yourself you can be friends with other people." Realizing this, the healthy person who wishes can begin by trying to understand why he rejects others; in so doing, he can start to change his own attitudes. We underline *healthy,* for Group Conversation is not planned to work primarily with the psychologically crippled person, ill with deep and serious conflicts. This is the province of the psychotherapist. However, for most of us "normals," Group Conversation can invoke experiences which have important emotional reference. Their sharing can give creative release and, like all creative experiences, may have therapeutic effect.

Laurens van der Post speaks of race prejudice as a form of self-rejection. The individual who cannot accept himself cannot accept others because he projects his hatred and fear of certain aspects of his own nature onto others. Thus the problem of race prejudice is interpreted as the rejection of oneself reflected in others who in turn tend to look for still others to reject whom they feel are below

77

them in the social order; and so the rejection goes on from individual to individual and from group to group.

This self-rejection is a part of the loss of identity about which psychologists and others are concerned today. Undoubtedly there was something of this in the violent reactions of some Polish and Lithuanian Americans in Chicago when challenged by the open-housing nonviolent marchers in 1967 led by Dr. Martin Luther King, Jr., and in the anti-Negro violence of the Italian-American students in a Brooklyn high school, which in turn fostered more hatred in the blacks. The prejudiced attitude of many white Southerners also fits into this pattern of self-rejection causing hatred of the other. The South is the only part of our country to have ever suffered defeat in a major war. Not only did this result in almost irreparable psychological as well as economic damage, but Southerners have been either looked down upon or romanticized by Americans from other regions. One understands the resentments and fears of many white Southerners as well as Northerners; but today we need to learn ways to develop mutual understanding not only between whites and Negroes all over the country but between white Northerners and Southerners, and thus break the cycle of hatred and release the spirit of cooperation in our common American life.

We have only to look within ourselves to see how difficult it is to apply to our own thinking and feeling an understanding of this self-rejection–projection process. We who have assumed the role of leadership of Group Conversation have encouraged each other to seek professional help in understanding our own attitudes and actions toward others. For instance, when we Americans, both whites and blacks, face the historical facts of slavery, civil war, reconstruction, lynching and civic injustice, and finally today slums and poverty, we ask ourselves, What are we to do about our guilt feelings? Depth psychology tells us that creative, mature action in facing and acting on today's problems comes not by loading onto these problems our feelings of personal guilt. In that way we may become immobilized. Real guilt usually comes only out of our real life situations. The individual's commitment and action emerge when they are not held back by his sense of guilt. These individual problems must be resolved before our inner energies are to be freed to work in creative, effective ways on our social problems. For instance, if we have a guilt feeling in relation to our mother or some

family member, it would be better to work out that particular relationship in an honest way and not make a race or social problem
out of what is basically a personal one.

At the Friends Center Workshop, we took the advice of some of
our black friends: "The best thing you can do now is to work on
your own attitudes." But can we perhaps hasten the coming of this
psychological freedom in ourselves and others through a group approach? We asked ourselves this question and knew we could find
the answer only by experimenting. We offer here our first faltering
steps in the use of Group Conversation in helping people to understand their own attitudes. We offer it with a plea that others also
experiment, feeling with van der Post that "there is a new kind of
human being living ahead of the meaning of our time and knowing
that the meaning has to be lived before it can be really known."

In a Southern City

SITUATION: Some members of the Religious Society of Friends
in a North Carolina city, aware that the attitudes of most blacks
toward whites have in the last decade been radically changed, asked
for help in looking at and understanding their own attitudes. In the
series of sessions, whites first met alone and later with blacks. In
other situations, whites and Negroes participated in all sessions.
When Negroes were present, they were asked to be frank and honest
in helping to bring about understanding of how each other felt, for
in the past there had seldom been an honest sharing of feeling between whites and blacks.

TOPIC: Toward Understanding Our Own Racial Attitudes.

LEAD QUESTIONS:

1. Share memories of early contacts with persons of other races.
Were the contacts with adults or children? Were they pleasant or
unpleasant?

2. By what experiences did our early environment give us feelings of superiority or inferiority, paternalism or overdependence?

3. Share adult contacts we have had with whites and blacks.
Are these relationships based on mature or childlike attitudes toward others? Do we find ourselves saying "All Negroes (or all
whites) are undependable" when we have many times experienced
the opposite? Do we find ourselves saying "All whites (or all
blacks) are dishonest" when we know through experience those

who have suffered for their honesty? In what situations, if any, do we feel inferior but act in an opposite way?

4. Have any of us had experiences of being shocked out of our apathy or prejudice? Does the experience of Sarah Patton Boyle, as related in her book, *The Desegregated Heart,** say anything to us? (She is the Virginian who took steps to change her own racial attitude. Here a co-leader gave a brief account of what Mrs. Boyle did.)

CLOSING: Since the kind of questions we asked ourselves were answered more easily and with greater honesty in group silence, this type of session usually closed with group meditation.

In an Upstate New York City

SITUATION: To try to establish a means of communication, 22 concerned individual white people, not previously active in race relations, met for two successive evenings—first alone, to look at their own attitudes, and then the second evening with more-or-less militant Negroes. At the end of these sessions the group was able to plan together toward community social action.

TOPIC: School Days.

LEAD QUESTIONS:

1. My favorite teacher—her looks, her room, the most inspiring thing I learned from her.

2. My worst teacher—brief account of the unjust ways in which I felt she treated me, and my response. Did this injustice affect my personality development?

REPORT: A few shared experiences in the group which helped toward mutual understanding and acceptance, as reported by a participant. One, who had been a white slum child, frequently found herself in disgrace with her first teachers. She transferred to another school where a teacher treated her with affection, confidence and respect; years later, she was still able to declare in wide-eyed surprise that "no one had ever treated me that way before." She had seen herself as her teachers had seen her.

The little Negro girl, now grown, had always been sent to school scrubbed, polished, pressed, and in starched collars and cuffs; she understood that this was her hard-laboring mother's effort to dispel the white teacher's and children's attitude that "Negroes are dirty,"

---

* (New York, William Morrow, 1962).

and to make her acceptable. The child observed the "other children" were casually dressed, and she felt conspicuous. Parents, she said, are still doing this today.

Another black participant from the South said, "I wanted to become a social worker, but my high school counselor said, 'No one ever heard of a Negro social worker. I advise you to forget it.' It took me ten years to get my degree in social work, but I got it."

CLOSING: Some of the comments in the discussion, held after coffee—

"Textbooks should be rewritten and should include the history of the hardships, growing pains, successes and contributions of our multi-ethnic groups. But because of the black people's long enslavement, poverty and social rejection, special immediate emphasis should be given this group. A Negro History Day (or Week) is inadequate."

A high spot in the discussion came when one Negro said: "Don't ask a black person, 'What can I do for you?' Ask yourselves what you can do for yourselves in changing your attitudes toward him. He is a human being who wants to become all that he is capable of becoming."

A white person asked himself, "Why should I miss his companionship—or a chance to know his vital response to being alive?"

"Some black people, especially the millions who are forced to live in ghettos, see the need to create their own school curriculum, and run their own educational systems. They feel that the education of their children, with whites making all the decisions, has been a disastrous failure, with everyone suffering from it."

In the Nation's Capital

SITUATION: In February 1968, an integrated group of 28 people had taken training in four weekend workshops to use Group Conversation in a Washington suburb to help build a more hospitable social climate for the coming of the nation's poor to Resurrection City. At the end of their workshop the participants wanted to look at their own attitudes with a practicing depth-psychologist who could help them come to a deeper understanding of their own racial anxieties.

TOPIC: Darkness and the Unknown.

PLACING: Where did we live as a child—city, suburb or farm?

LEAD QUESTIONS:

1. What were our early experiences of being put to bed: bedtime stories; lullabies; fear of dark, bogeyman, witches, ghosts— what did they look like? Did we have prayers—"Now I lay me" or others? When did we meet the idea of death? of the Great Unknown? Did we fear animals or strangers? For whom was darkness a beautiful mystery—stars and dark night—full of adventure?

2. As we were growing up, and as teenagers or later, did we have experiences of relating to the unknown, to the new, strange or different? Example: Did our family move to a new neighborhood? Our first experience in camp.

3. As adults, how do we now react to the new, the unknown, the strange?

4. Since we want to look at our own feelings about the opposite race: What were some of our first experiences? Are our memories of these experiences warm and pleasant or fearful? Do we remember our family entertaining a guest of the opposite race in our home?

5. What playmate experiences do we have? Did we as children often visit the home of a child of another race? As adults, do we visit in their homes? Was the relationship strictly business or warmly personal? What experiences can we share?

CLOSING: Our psychologist said that "many of us tend to think of the unknown as dangerous, evil, possibly terrifying. Others of us think of it as a mystery containing possible adventure and beauty. How can we help ourselves and others to separate the dark and ominous from the light and beautiful shadow in our lives?— for our shadow can be both light and dark, and it has nothing to do with skin color. When we can do this, we can venture forth claiming for ourselves in our friendships what really belongs to us."

In a Northern City

SITUATION: A small integrated group of Group Conversation leaders in a Northern city, inspired by the writings of Laurens van der Post * in which he gives vivid examples, in both individual and national life, of the rejection-projection psychological process, decided to explore together this concept as it applied to themselves.

* *The Dark Eye in Africa,* (New York, William Morrow and Co., 1955); *Venture to the Interior,* (New York, William Morrow and Co., 1951); *Race Prejudice as Self-Rejection* (Workshop for Cultural Democracy, 1958).

They hoped that this exploration would not only enable them to be more perceptive leaders of Group Conversation but would result in deepening their own interpersonal relationships. They also hoped it would enable them to find and build meaningful friendships with people of groups other than their own with more honesty and freedom.

In their planned sessions they used several group methods, moving from one to the other: sharing experiences which would have some relationship to the rejection-projection concept, utilizing book reviews and quotations related to the subject, and finally group discussion and group meditation.

In preparation for the first session, each was given the following quotation from van der Post for his at-home meditation:

> We all live in an age of essentially displaced people . . . We have lost the inner sense of belonging. We have lost it partly because we have thought that through the physical objects of life, through the material side of life we could solve our problems . . . In Africa [van der Post was born in South Africa of English and Dutch parents and now lives in England] we get this problem of displacement in its most dramatic form. There we call it detribalization, and I speak to you now as one who is perhaps more detribalized than most . . . Our whole way of living is so much a rejection of the natural, the feeling, the warm, the human being, that we keep nature in a little box of its own.

SESSION ONE: informal discussion.

TOPIC: Feelings of Belonging in Our Family and in Our Community. (Taking the two threads in our quotation from van der Post—our need for a sense of belonging and "keeping in a box" the feeling, the warm, the natural part of our being, let us share our related experiences.)

PLACING: Where did we grow up? Give a brief sentence about our sibling relationships.

LEAD QUESTIONS:

1. Were there in our family spontaneous expressions of love between adults, and between adults and children? Was there also free expression of anger in quarreling?

2. Were we in a family where anything could happen spontane-

ously? What for instance? Were others of us in a well-ordered, structured family where things happened according to schedule? How did we feel? Did we conform or rebel?

3. Did our family have close relationships with neighbors? Do we have a feeling of belonging when we think of the community in which our early life was spent? Or do we too feel detribalized? When we were about ten, did we visit a friend's family just because they were different?

4. Can we recall early experiences of intense wonderment about the universe? Were we usually alone or with others during these experiences, i.e. seeing stars at night, or the lights in a city street in the rain? Did we share with adults or peers these wonderments?

> . . . The great need of our time is somehow to get rid of the pretence, this awful secrecy in life, where people profess to be one thing and live another. Somehow that has to be brought out in the open, so that we will stop pushing the natural part of ourselves into a corner. We have slums in the spirit just as we have them in cities.

> . . . . We are *frightened* because we might feel too free. Heaven knows what we are going to do next when we let life in on that scale. We might even stop going into Parliament. One might just like to sit in the sun all day. One might become so natural he might love everybody. It would be disastrous. So we push it, we fight it, we push it away all the time . . .

> But the things we have rejected are the things which the dark man in Africa implicitly accepts as basic.

Does anything from these quotations ring a bell in our experiences in this country? the American Negro of the past generation? the American Indian? the flower people of this generation?

CLOSING: This session ended with unguided discussion over coffee after which the following quotations were distributed in preparation for the next session:

> The black person whom we persecute is the natural, the spontaneous, the intuitive person. We are in a state of profound civil war, and one of the most terrible things to me, as I look back upon the history of Africa and the world, is that I

see that this spiritual damage which we have done to ourselves is a spiritual damage that we have done also to Africa. One of the greatest mistakes that we made was to think that the natural man is not the spiritual man. The white man in Africa has never recognized that he has something important to learn from the blacks. When my English and Dutch ancestors 300 years ago went to Africa, the black was ready to welcome them, but now his eye is dark toward us.

An old hunter I knew as a boy, said to me: "This conflict that you have is caused by only one thing and that is that the natural man *is* and the unnatural man *has*. Those are the two things that are at war in the modern world. It is this problem of having and this problem of being.

SESSION TWO: Book review; Group Conversation; poetry reading.

A brief book review: The story, *Venture to the Interior,* tells of a man who loses his life in an accident. One person in the party had an intuitive feeling that such a thing might happen, but did not share his feeling.

TOPIC: Looking at Our Own Spontaneity and Intuition.

PLACING: Recall some imaginative or spontaneous thing we did as a child.

LEAD QUESTIONS:

1. Are we as spontaneous now as we were as a child? Can we recall any pressure from our environment to act differently, which might have started the cut-off from our spontaneity?

2. What experiences of intuition, whether significant or not, have we had at any age? Did we act on them or reject them?

3. What memories have we of a rejection of a part of ourselves? (Share actual *incidents* as much as possible.) As girls did we ever wish we were boys? As boys who had intuitive feelings or wonderment, were we too embarrassed to express them? Did we ever wish we were members of a cultural group other than our own?

The leader put the seeking of the group into these words: "In the subconscious all these qualities run together, like waters in the ocean. We can all draw on these forces, but if our culture calls a boy a sissy, if he expresses his intuitive and wonderment feelings, then he tends to reject that part of himself, but projects it upon all girls and considers them weaklings."

4. Can we share any experiences of our own which may throw light on this idea? We do not need to agree—we are trying to understand.

5. Who can put into words based on our own experiences how some modern sophisticates tend to reject in themselves the feeling, the warm, the spontaneous, and then project those feelings on the unsophisticated black, calling him emotional, childish?

6. Is this spontaneity related to what we mean by freedom? by "black is beautiful"? by "soul force"?

7. If in our friendships any of us are free now of a sense of skin color, was there a particular time when we *knew* we were free?

CLOSING: This session ended with reading poetry related to blackness. (See Bibliography.)

In preparation for Session Three the following quotation was distributed:

> We see confusion with the image in our own minds, and until one comes to that point and to that realization, we are not really free of what I call color prejudice. Once you have seen it, once you have realized it, the whole thing goes up in smoke. Immediately you become free, free to like the person who is likeable, whatever his color, and to dislike the person who is dislikeable, whatever his color. This is the real freedom.
>
> But we must face up first of all to what it is *in ourselves* that we reject that makes us reject a person who mirrors our own rejection in the outer world. . . .

SESSION THREE: Group Conversation; meditation.

TOPIC: "It's the not-me in thee which makes thee precious to me." The need to learn from each other. (The next step after absorbing van der Post's plea to learn from each other took us into looking at the quantity and quality of our friendships with Americans of various ethnic backgrounds.)

PLACING: Briefly share an early experience of being a pal to someone quite different from ourselves.

LEAD QUESTIONS: What were some of the things we did together? Did adults object? Was it later in life that this experience came to us? Do we have or take opportunities to experience today customs and values in other groups which may be different from our own?

Some in the group had participated in Indian pow-wows, Jewish Seders, Negro churches, Soul Food restaurants, theater and dance, and Chinese New Year parades. The participants, both whites and blacks, asked themselves if they had had any experiences similar to those Ralph Ellison, who grew up in a segregated community in Oklahoma City, writes about:

> Culturally this people represents one of the many subcultures which make up that great amalgam of European and native American cultures which is the culture of the United States. This "American Negro Culture" is expressed in a body of folk lore, in the musical forms of the spirituals, the blues and jazz; an idiomatic version of American speech (especially in Southern United States); a cuisine; a body of dance forms, and even a dramaturge which is generally unrecognized as such because it is still tied to the more folkish Negro churches. Some Negro preachers are great showmen. It must be pointed out, however, that due to the loose links which Negro Americans have with the rest of the nation, these cultural expressions are constantly influencing the larger body of American culture and are in turn influenced by them.

There was much informal sharing of experiences and discussion. The one in the group who had formed friendships with a few American Indians reacted to the following quotation of Aldous Huxley in his book *Ends and Means:* *

> Is it possible for us to acquire from the Zuñi Indians their admirable habit of non-attachment to wealth and personal success, and at the same time to preserve our intellectual alertness, our interest in science, our capacity for making rapid technological progress and social change? These are questions which it is impossible to answer with any degree of confidence. Only experience and deliberate experiment can tell us if our problem can be completely solved.

Have these Indians held on to these qualities today? Since we do not know, what kind of exploration would help us find the answer? Where can we find contacts with Indians if none live in our community? What books might we read? Should we at this point

* (New York, Harper & Bros., 1937).

ask ourselves if any of this self-rejection–projection psychological process applies to the way whites have felt and treated Negroes, Indians, Mexicans, Puerto Ricans and Orientals?

CLOSING: This session closed with a lengthy group meditation inspired by the following quotation from van der Post:

> Go to the place inside of ourselves where we truly belong— in the natural or the unsophisticated part of ourselves. What is it in ourselves that we reject, that makes us reject a person who mirrors our own rejection in the outer world? We fight against it as bad, even though we are secretly attracted to it. And since the dark-skinned man has it more than we do we fight against him . . . He provokes the natural in us and we are terrified of the natural . . . we are frightened because we might feel too free . . . one might become so natural he might *love everybody!*
>
> . . . If black and white do not get together and meet inwardly and outwardly on friendly terms, there may occur an event on a world scale symbolized by the story of the white and black knights in King Arthur's Court:
>
>> There were two brothers, the Black Knight and White Knight and they set off on a quest, each on his own, one going north and one south. After many years they met in a dark wood and did not recognize each other. They immediately assumed they were enemies and when both were lying bleeding to death on the grass, they undid their helmets and recognized they were brothers.
>
> This legend illustrates in its deepest sense the problem of rejection—a rejection in ourselves, in society, and in civilization . . . To find ways to learn and accept from each other is the most urgent issue of our desperate age—if we are not to end in world disaster.

In a Northern Suburban High School

SITUATION: By the academic year of 1968-69, rebellion on the campuses as a response to frustrations, hostilities and lack of trust or communication between groups of students, faculty and administration, reached many high schools throughout the country. New Rochelle, a New York City suburb, experienced two student strikes —one seeking official recognition of Martin Luther King's birthday (the first after his death), another led by white Protestant and Jewish intellectuals demanding removal of police from the campus.

More important than the expressed demands were the underlying feelings of black hostility and suspicion of whites, neglect by the other students of black and Italian-American student needs and hopes, and joint student mistrust of the administration and faculty. In an attempt to deal with these feelings, a group of students requested a day of encounter groups for all students and faculty. At the end of the day, with a selected group of students and faculty, there was to be a demonstration of how Group Conversation could be used in conjunction with encounter groups to help student leaders look at a more constructive way to use anger.

Social workers from the community were invited in to lead the four-hour-long encounter groups with faculty as observers. A few student statements follow:

> There are tensions here not only between blacks and whites but between teachers and students.

> The teachers and the Board of Education are not democratic in their relationships with us.

> That assembly in honor of Dr. King was turned into something he didn't stand for. It created hostility on both sides.

> A basketball game turned into a fight. My mother was there and she was terrified.

> Now everybody is angry and we say mean things about each other but we only reflect the divisions in our city.

TOPIC: Anger and Closeness—Past, Present and Future
LEAD QUESTIONS:

1. Describe briefly the atmosphere of our early home: Were there many adult anxieties and angers? Were they expressed or repressed?

2. What about our own anger today—in home? at school? How is it expressed? How does it feel?

3. Feelings of closeness to others: toward siblings, parents, pets, pals. The feeling of "falling in love."

THE SHARING: The group of 30 students and faculty freely shared the nature of their early home atmospheres—the usual sibling quarrels and parental disagreements. Two sisters looked like twins and hence got involved in each other's quarrels. A boy feeling lonely in his home grew very close to his dog: "It's odd how close I feel to that dog and how good that closeness feels." One girl shared her "low-down" feeling when even now she's torn emotionally between her divorce-getting parents. The feeling released in the following group silence showed the girl that she was even now receiving the sympathetic support she needed. And then the mood was lightened by a radiating warmth when—in answer to the question "How does it feel to be really close to another?"—a high-school senior boy sitting next to his sweetheart expressed the wonder of being in love for the first time.

CLOSING: The dynamics of the group moved the process into an encounter between the students and faculty as to their feelings about each other and the school. Since, apparently, this was the need uppermost in their feelings, no effort was made by the leader to channel the group toward looking at their experiences of anger and closeness which would have followed logically. Flexibility and spontaneity are built into Group Conversation.

Brief excerpts follow from the challenging dialogue between the students and faculty:

A teacher—"I am concerned that such a large number of students (one-third) felt so alienated that they could not attend our encounter groups this morning."

A student—"Teachers should have attended, too, for some have wrong attitudes."

A young teacher—"We do not have enough time to know each other as persons. I wish students could feel comfortable by using first names with us."

A student—"We've had this good experience today but tomorrow we have to go right back into the same old atmosphere. You walk into a classroom and you just get taught—the bell rings and you leave—it's all so boring."

A teacher—"I think we have here the beginning of change. You (16 students) have found that you can approach the teachers and administration for they are represented here."

A student—"Could we ever have a Summerhill-oriented high

school? Learning is more in the living than in just sitting in class-rooms."

A young teacher sums up the dialogue—"If we are really serious about all this then it's necessary for experiences such as we've had today to become an integral part of the regular program."

OBSERVATIONS: One psychological point of view becoming in-creasingly popular in our time encourages the freedom to express anger, even though it may have destructive consequences. Another viewpoint, presented by Dr. Ira Progoff, is that "the anger in our time has something to say to us. It is clearing the way for a next step in our development. Therefore we must not give vent to it as a psychological dumping, but we must try to reach behind it to what it is trying to tell us." *

Could it be that the anger felt in this school is related to the out-moded educational system in most of our public schools which steals from us the opportunity for personal growth for which we hunger? What does the answer to this question say to us as stu-dents and as faculty by way of action and responsibility for our action?

The leader might observe that in another situation this discussion could generate a question about the tremendous amount of social anger in our country and in the world today—the expressions this social anger takes against social injustices. Can this social anger be used for societal growth? Can this force be controlled? Is there a new kind of relationship trying to be born between individuals and between groups in society as a whole? Do we have intimations of what that relationship might be? A modern seer has this to say:

> . . . if in dealing with the problem of the various human races, their appearance, their awakening, their future, we start from its purely biological roots, it will lead us to recognize that the only climate in which man can continue to grow is that of devotion and self-denial in a spirit of brotherhood. In truth, at the rate the consciousness and the ambitions of the world are increasing, it will explode unless it learns to love. The fu-ture of the thinking earth is organically bound up with the turning of the forces of hate into forces of charity.**

* Dr. Ira Progoff in an unpublished lecture at Friends Conference on Re-ligion and Psychology in 1969.
** Pierre Teilhard de Chardin, *Hymn of the Universe* (New York, Harper & Row, 1961).

6

Uniting People for
Community Needs

WHAT IS NEEDED TODAY, in many parts of our country, are more opportunities for a community-wide use of this unique Group Conversation method, by relating it to other group methods so that all or most of the individuals' social worlds—the home, school, church and place of work—will relate to the same goal, i.e., equal opportunities for all Americans as we work together to solve our problems of living together.

Many projects of this sort, especially in Office of Economic Opportunity funded projects, are being conducted. So often, however, these projects do not tend to move communities forward as a whole, for they have been too fragmented and unrelated in their social action activities. So often, too, there have not been, in many situations, enough funds for local leaders to make this all-community approach. Now, with certain anti-poverty programs expressing, and with policy makers articulating the need for total involvement of a community and for including the poor in decision-making for plans affecting their lives, we present here a brief account of four of the several projects we have engaged in, and a fifth which is in the planning stage. Local leaders will realize that the use of Group Conversation is a part of an ongoing process of aiding individuals

92

of various kinds of backgrounds to believe in one another as persons, so that they will make the attempt to work together more productively, whether as community workers, volunteers for social action projects, talented suburbanites, welfare recipients, or concerned parents.

Motivating Social Action Volunteers

SITUATION: The Ecumenical Task Force in a Northern city set up a committee to prepare themselves and others to use effective ways to involve mainly middle-class whites and blacks in becoming active as volunteers in the civil rights struggle and other social action programs in the community.

First step: training workshops in the use and follow-up of Group Conversation. Thirty persons of different races, sexes and backgrounds—Catholic nuns, Protestant pastors, public school teachers, and housewives.

Second step: follow-up. After their training, each team of two recruited their own participants for a five-session, weekly series of meetings in their own homes, using Group Conversation followed by discussion. This led to the involvement of many participants as volunteers in several social action projects.

TOPICS (used in the home meetings, with one session on each):

1. *Becoming acquainted.*

2. *Our own prejudices*—to recognize them in our past and present experiences.

3. *Institutional racism*—to understand how the system works and what it does to us.

4. *Black consciousness and Black Power*—to understand and respond creatively.

5. *What we can do*—to see institutionalized racism where we are and to design strategy to overcome it.

LEAD QUESTIONS:

Our own prejudices. Introduction by leader: Psychologists generally agree on two main causes of prejudices, one being simply that most children tend to imitate the prejudices of their parents and other adults. Later these persons may throw off such prejudices when they move in other kinds of social worlds or acquire facts showing the untruth of their prejudice. The second cause of prejudice is more serious, for it feeds demands of a personality frustrated in childhood to such an extent that it gains satisfaction in bruising others by acting out their prejudices. (Note to leader: Postpone the discussion of these theories now. Look first at their own experiences.)

1. Earliest memories of being given a sense of importance by grown-ups. Did any of them seem to pick us out and give us praise for something? How did we feel?

2. If we did not get such praise and attention, do we recall doing something on our own to gain attention? Were we punished for any of this? Did we feel we were unjustly punished?

3. How did we treat other children, siblings or neighborhood friends? Were we ever the bully, or were we at the mercy of a bully?

4. Did we have normal or above-normal feelings of being lonely or frustrated? What did we do about it? (Note to leader: Do not allow participants to voice any informal analyses of other participants. This is *not* group therapy.)

5. Can we admit any prejudices we may have now toward groups of people? Have any of us succeeded in overcoming prejudices? What societal frustrations hit us today: Vietnam war? Escalating prices? Racial crises? Can we share any personal frustration or disillusionment?

6. What is meant by scapegoating?

CLOSING: What is it that helps us to live with our frustrations, rather than hurting others? Can we share our philosophy of life, some inspiring words, or special hope in the future?

Institutional racism. Introduction by leader: Without defining racism at this point, let us look at the main institutions we have been a part of since birth—home, school, church and business.

1. What was our earliest contact in our home with people from other races, religions, countries? Were these contacts on a basis of mutual respect, equality, even of appreciation and love? As a child did we feel differently about these contacts than did our parents or other adults?

2. What experiences come back, showing that as children we were "open" to the different person or the stranger? Did we express these feelings? Or did we conform and finally come to feel the same way as so many of the adults around us felt? Can we ask similar questions about our experiences in school, church or synagogue, and in the business world?

Black consciousness and Black Power. To respond creatively is to strive to restrain, at least temporarily, whatever adverse feelings we may have toward anyone, to try to put ourselves into his shoes, to *feel* with him. If we can do this as whites in our relationships with blacks, perhaps some new, *creative* ideas about black consciousness and Black Power may be engendered within us. Because music and poetry are so effective in strengthening these positive and potentially creative feelings, we utilized such recordings as these:

> *Big Bill Broonzy Sings Folk Songs,* FA2328A and FG-3586B, Folkways Records (165 West 46th Street, New York, N.Y.).

> *The Glory of Negro History,* narrated by Langston Hughes, FC7752A, Folkways Records.

> Tapes and recordings of sermons and addresses of Dr. Martin Luther King, Jr., available from Martin Luther King Speaks, Inc., 260 Audubon Avenue, Suite 32G, New York, N.Y. 10033.

What can we do? How can we prepare ourselves? Do we need to deepen our spiritual roots? to understand and control our own feelings, especially anger?

DISCUSSION RESOURCES: These thought- and discussion-provoking materials were given to the Ecumenical Task Force leaders for suggested use with their participants. Additional sources of similar materials will be found in the Bibliography.

1. Statement of Jesus: "I am the vine, ye are the branches." What other biblical statements assure us that all peoples are a part of one organic whole, and therefore when one part suffers, all parts suffer? How is this universal truth expressed in other faiths—Judaism, Buddhism, Taoism? Teilhard de Chardin rejoices that, because of modern technological and scientific advances, there is a gradual combining of individuals and races. "The only climate in which man can continue to grow," he observes, "is that of devotion and self-denial in a spirit of brotherhood; in truth, at the rate that the consciousness and the ambitions of the world are increasing, it will explode unless it learns to love."

Are we trying to radiate these or similar spiritual truths to all around us in words which they can understand? This may demand special efforts to share these truths as never before with our close friends and relatives. Can we engage strangers on buses, on sidewalks, in parks, or anywhere in such conversations?

2. When our white friends express anger against *all* blacks because of the violent actions of some blacks, it is wise to permit the anger to be expressed, but to try to redirect it against the true causes of our frustrations and anger today—the war, high taxation, inadequate incomes to meet family needs, social injustices of all kinds. How can anger be channeled for personal and societal growth via "righteous indignation"?

Whenever we bring friends and acquaintances together in formal or informal groups, perhaps in purely social gatherings in our homes, we can utilize the occasion to help them develop a better understanding of the plight of our Negro, Puerto Rican, Indian, Mexican and Oriental citizens. We should forearm ourselves with facts and present them in whatever ways are most natural and effective for us to use.

It could be pointed out, for example, that most race riots occur in city ghettos. Do we really know what it is like to be forced to live under ghetto conditions? We should have at our fingertips data such as these about Newark, N.J. (or other similar ghetto cities, preferably ones as close to home as possible):

> Newark has the highest crime rate, the highest tuberculosis and maternal mortality rate, the highest substandard housing rate for any city its size in the country, and the lowest per capita income. The unemployment rate is 8.2% as against 3.8% for the rest of the country. In the ninth to twelfth grades, the dropout rate is 32%. [These data worsened after the Ecumenical Task Force sessions were held.]

Nothing done in the past twenty years has directly touched the plight and hardships of the majority of blacks—not the civil rights marches, nor the recent enactment of civil rights laws, nor the several court decisions that have undergirded the legislation. These positive forces still have not removed the roots of the hopelessness and despair felt by blacks. We should not attempt to apologize for or excuse the episodes of violence; but we should explain the causes to our friends, and remind them that responsible Negro leaders assert that 95% of the blacks oppose rioting. Do we know the names of these leaders? read their writings, or printed interviews? go to meetings where they are speaking? Shouldn't we seek such leaders out in our own communities and offer them whatever help they need and want from us?

3. In these discussions with our friends we should be prepared to present facts about valuable contributions blacks have made to American life and to western culture generally. Such examples serve to reveal the potentials which our faith in them and our giving them truly equal opportunities could release among blacks. Beyond citing outstanding Negroes, we can point to the fact that the unpaid labor of black slaves helped to transform the Southern wilderness into prosperous plantations some two hundred years earlier than whites alone could have done it. We can also cite the musical contributions which have permeated our culture: spirituals, jazz, blues, folk songs, and much of the rock and folk-rock music of the younger generation. Many of the lyrics reflect a profound sense of social injustices and "establishment" hypocrisy, and often at the same time reveal great hopes for changes today and tomorrow.

4. Bring into the open our own fears as well as those of others, relating to major areas of life.

Work. Do we unconsciously fear the economic competition when blacks and other minority groups are given equal employment opportunities? If so, we should understand that the chief causes of general unemployment are inadequate educational preparation for jobs, dislocations caused by automation which necessitate job retraining, the reduction of buying power caused by inflation, increased taxation, high interest rates for loans and home mortgages, etc.—all of which apply equally to white and black youth and adults.

Education. Do we fear the lowering of educational standards for our children when *de facto* school segregation is eradicated? Our far-seeing educators insist that this need not be so if we will give adequate financial support for enrichment programs, sufficient guidance counseling personnel, and remedial specialists to pull the disadvantaged students up to the level of the advantaged. This, they maintain, can provide good quality education for *all* pupils.

Marriage. Do we fear the possibility of intermarriage if blacks become completely integrated into all phases of American life? There is, of course, no biological reason to prevent intermarriage. Much race mixing has already taken place in American life, most of it prior to the Civil War. Statistics show that there is less now, but sociologists observe that new attitudes toward intermarriage are emerging, particularly among the younger generation. It is both a cultural and a sociological problem. What is needed is more pre-marital counseling and better education in family life so that any marriage will have a better chance of being successful.

EARLY RESULTS (as reported by the coordinator):

"Home" groups often went on informally for hours after the evening's Group Conversation was over. For many participants, this was their first experience in an interracial social situation.

One white woman, born in England and married to an American Negro, said, "I never knew people could be so nice. People have acted so awful to me since I've been married."

A black who grew up in Harlem told a group the story of his childhood. His sharing of these memories was so effective that the group decided to start a Street Academy in their city in coopera-tion with the city's Youth Board.

In the sixth week, all "home" group members were convened in a large meeting room. Almost immediately, 75 people signed up for local volunteer work; examples: some participated in the Street Academy; some surveyed pricing practices in local supermarkets; some helped to organize a center for welfare mothers. A leadership training workshop for volunteers won 30 recruits.

ONGOING RESULTS: A teenage coffee house; a series of Catho-lic-Protestant dialogues; a continuing Group Conversation training program in a Presbyterian church. [Most volunteers are still work-ing in the various projects which they joined.]

Training Southern Rural Negroes

SITUATION: A local affiliate of the Southern Christian Leader-ship Conference, in an Alabama county, received an OEO grant for a family development program. It had three major thrusts: a basic adult education program, a child care program with mothers' classes, and a youth enrichment program. The programs were de-signed to work with seasonal farm working families, on a county-wide basis. To initiate the staff, a three-week screening and training program was set up.

Eighty Negroes came from various parts of the county. Some were high school graduates; a few had attended or graduated from Southern Negro colleges; most had a meager elementary educa-tion. The trainees came on their own time and at their own expense, knowing that only about forty were to be selected to be salaried teachers or aids in child care centers, youth work centers and adult education programs. Involved in the training of these people were specialists in communication, nutrition, planned parenthood, child development and basic adult education.

For the first three-week-long workshop we chose Group Conversation as a vehicle for training in group leadership, for several reasons. The most important quality for successful teaching in this program would be communication skills. Repeated experience in Group Conversation meant that the participants would grow to have confidence that their contributions were valuable. They also would learn that others had a great deal to contribute, and that this give-and-take can be exciting. We found that these experiences aided immeasurably in breaking down the authoritarian idea of education most of the trainees had previously.

A slightly different series of Group Conversations was developed for those trainees seeking adult education and youth leader positions than for those interested in day care. For example, the adult education trainees moved more quickly from family experience to school and work experience, as these were more relevant to their anticipated jobs. Ideas for lead questions for the modified Group Conversations: (1) first school, (2) best teacher, (3) first job, (4) meaningful work (or learning), (5) punishments and rewards.

The day's schedule for both groups consisted of: (1) Group Conversation sessions; (2) assembly to report on insights they had achieved; (3) lunch; (4) lecture on "Early Childhood Education" by a professor of education, bringing out needed concepts on rejection and acceptance, identification, and civil rights; (5) buzz sessions (sometimes these were given over to the use of role-play or psycho-drama).

SESSION ONE.

GOAL: For those preparing for Child Care Centers to show the relevance of their own early experiences to the needs of young children today. (To do this we made the adaptation of going back and forth in our sharing from our own memories to what could be done today with children in day care centers.)

TOPIC: Our Earliest Childhood Memories.

PLACING: Name and where we grew up.

LEAD QUESTIONS:

1. Since psychologists tell us of the child's deep need for love and a sense of belonging, what is our own memory of being loved (rocked or petted) as a small child? What do we remember of being tucked into bed? (Lullabies and prayers were shared with the feelings we still remembered.) What does all this tell us about what to do today in child care centers? (Some thought they might well learn some lullabies. After a brief discussion we returned to our own experiences.)

2. What memories do we have of feeling close to the family around the dining table? Every day? Once a week? Bible-reading? Story-telling? Grace? Do these memories suggest activities for to-day's child care centers?

3. Besides memories of being loved and accepted, we have memories of being rejected. Who punished us? Did we reject ourselves— think we were ugly, too short or tall? How did we express these feelings? Anger, revenge?

Discussion: How does all this affect the child's developing personality? What does this tell us about our treatment of children in our own families, in child care centers, and in our youth program?

SESSION TWO
GOALS:
1. To help day care teachers develop good meal times for the children.   •
2. To help youth and adult teachers in their search for a means of making home and family life more meaningful for each member.
3. To show the value to the developing child for the family to have regular times when members can feel close, i.e., can have emotionally satisfying times together. These can come during the daily or weekly special meals.

TOPIC: Special Meals in Our Family.

PLACING: Give name and say which was our favorite meal.

LEAD QUESTIONS: Give word picture of our family at the table. If both parents worked outside the home, when did the family eat together? Who cooked? Special dishes? What activities at table: Grace? Conversation? Did we or did we not feel close to each other at the table? How did we learn manners? Too much emphasis? What special meals, as Thanksgiving, Christmas or birthday? Describe them.

DISCUSSION: What do these experiences tell us we might well

teach in child care centers today? Words and songs of grace? Should we celebrate special days and birthdays? How? Are "manners" different today? Learning to like new foods.

SESSION THREE.

GOAL: To examine the source of our inferiority feelings and of how we project on others what we reject within ourselves.

TOPICS (early experiences): Since all of us, growing up in the world of adults, took on some feelings of inferiority, can we share some of these early feelings about ourselves? Did we feel there was something the matter with us which kept others from liking us— too big, too little, too fat? What incidents were there when others did reject us? In what ways did we try to compensate? In what ways did adults help us feel accepted? Birthday parties, family or church picnics, Christmas festivities, etc.? Did these activities help us accept ourselves?

One person remembered what she now thinks was overcompensation in her home about cleanliness. *"We* are all dirty, *they* are all clean." "Oh, how we had to scrub! Now I think I have overcome at least that one bit of self-rejection. I know that *I* like being clean because it's a way of staying healthy and neat, but I don't have to be *overly* clean, and I can like you for what you *really* are, and not because you are or are not clean."

TOPIC (adult experiences): What do our own experiences tell us about the way we should treat children? Does adult approval and praise facilitate learning? What can we do now to overcome our self-rejection? Are the psychologists right in saying we must accept and love ourselves before we can accept and love others? How does this relate to the black-is-beautiful theme today? How do we want to deal with it today? Langston Hughes says how he feels in *My People:*

> *The night is beautiful,*
> *So the faces of my people.*
> *The stars are beautiful,*
> *So the eyes of my people.*
> *Beautiful, also, is the sun.*
> *Beautiful, also, are the souls of my people.*

A poem like this one gives us a warm feeling about "the people of color," but prize-winning American writer Ralph Ellison shows us that there is more to being a Negro than "high visibility: What makes you Negro is having grown up under certain cultural conditions, having undergone an experience that shapes your culture. There is a body of folk lore, a certain sense of American history; there is our psychology and the peculiar circumstances under which we have lived. There is our cuisine, though we don't admit it, and our forms of expression. I speak certain idioms; this is also part of the concord that makes me a Negro." (*New York Times,* 11/20/66)

Do we want to help each other use such information with others, or is it not relevant to life as we see it now?

SESSION FOUR.

GOAL: To take the same group further into rejection and acceptance.

TOPIC: Rewards and Punishments in our Youth.

LEAD QUESTIONS:

1. Who did the punishing in our family? Who was the authority figure (the boss) in the family? How did we feel about him or her? As we look back at the extreme strictness some of us experienced, was it ever for us a source of strength? Roland Hayes says in his autobiography that his mother was "severe but also righteous and strong . . . I needed then and later her support of steel." Is this need different today?

2. What of punishment at school? Were we afraid of any of our teachers? In Sunday school did the preacher or someone else "boss" us? What about the "white folks" in our county? Who was considered the "boss man"—the policeman, the sheriff, or someone else? What have been our experiences with him? What feelings did we have about him? Did any of us ever feel a sense of security at the policeman's presence? Is our feeling any different today?

3. We can see that we and our children are in the midst of change. Who should and can keep order in society today? Must each one find his own strength for inner discipline? What do we feel about punishment of children today? What do specialists in early-childhood education say? What do our own hearts tell us?

It was after this session that the total group, one afternoon, had a socio-drama related to their feelings about the way they were treated by the whites in their community. The experience they chose to role-play was that of a store owned by a white man who made Negroes stand and wait, sometimes for long periods, while he attended to the white customers. The socio-drama was a real catharsis for the group, followed by a valuable discussion about how best to handle such situations today.

SESSION FIVE.

GOAL: To deepen our own sense of self-identity and to see if we can help our children in that respect.

TOPIC: Our Names and What They Mean to Us.

PLACING: Our given name. Do we know why our parents selected it? Did we like the name as a child?

LEAD QUESTIONS:

1. What are our nicknames? pet names? Who gave us a pet name when we were little?

2. What names have we given our children? What are their pet names? Do these pet names help us to feel closer to our children? Do we—with our little children—play games which involve our senses—touch, etc.?

3. How can we help our children who are facing, and some already attending, integrated schools? Can we share here what some are going through? (Some were parents of such children in the county.) "White teachers make our children sit away from the class and never ask them to recite." "Other children trip them, spill ink on them, even beat them up on the playground, but teachers are never around to see what happens." "Worse things than that, my daughter tells me; but what's the use of talking about it?"

Another mother reported a recent meeting in her home with a Negro professor from a Northern university who was making a study of just such treatment: "Nine of our children who are in integrated schools met with him, and they told of the kind of things you've been saying, but the professor really inspired those kids. He supported their courage: 'I know it's awfully rough on you,' he told them, 'but don't you ever forget it's much worse for those white children. If we let them get away with this, we're helping them destroy the very core of their own humanity'." The leader took up that thread.

4. Can we help each other understand what it means to "destroy the core of our own humanity"? Some say that the creating and the singing of "the blues" have kept us from "losing our hu-

manity." Can we sing any now which hold up a glimmer of light in the midst of darkness? What about "I hate to see that evenin' sun go down"? What was our American dream? Has it gone completely? Who knows any part of Dr. King's speech "I have a dream"? What is our hope today?

RESULTS: The ensuing discussion revealed the ambivalence of the involved American Negro as he teeters between accepting the nonviolent or the violent approach to racism.

From a report of one of the trainers:

1. It is a bit difficult to separate final results from ongoing program since the trainees were so wonderful and brought such fresh enthusiasm and hope to every session. Some of our outstanding rewards were the experiences we had in training the job trainees to use the Group Conversation method themselves. This was done, at their request, on their weekend time, and after they had participated in many Group Conversation sessions as a part of their job training and screening. The ones who were chosen to be adult teachers and youth leaders later used the method in their own teaching.

2. The repeated experiences of recalling their own childhood memories were especially important for those with no formal education: *This re-experiencing freed them to do what their hearts told them to do.* They thus began *to feel* what was needed. This aided immeasurably in not only breaking down their authoritarian idea of education, but of the dominance of authority in other life activities. The long-emphasized supreme role of authority in work, in community participation and in child rearing and family interaction was modified in this series of Group Conversation experiences and allowed individuals to think of listening to their own ideas and consciences and to let their children do likewise. The implementation of the civil rights laws had begun to make some difference in breaking through this rigid way of life, but there was very little difference in their feeling about the change. Now it was as if, while the shell of the old authoritarian pattern of life began to shatter, they began to reach for new patterns to replace the changing ones and found them within their own spirits.

3. Some of the people involved in planning and executing this project became very excited about the use of Group Conversation as a *teaching vehicle* in this setting, in addition to its use as "a

tool for psychological conditioning in increasing communication between people and in easing the basic wariness with which we keep people at bay."

They were especially eager that a way be found to convey to the reader "the genius of the process for *teaching a 'feeling comprehension'*—the vistas it may open in helping one to comprehend the other by re-experiencing the emotional impact of one's own childhood experiences in similar settings. The idea that you may teach principles, reactions, feelings—in short, LIVING—rather than facts only, with Group Conversation has now come through as a separate conceptual entity." One of the ways this kind of teaching was accomplished was in moving from early memories to what the feelings about those memories mean when applied to situations that are faced by teachers, nursery workers and others today.

Moving a Group of Harlem Church Women

In this huge Harlem Church with its nine vested choirs, its several worship services each Sunday, its numerous work units through the week, they were the desperate, the dislocated, the forgotten. Though they celebrate communion with several thousand fellow members they share the friendship of few.

They had come from several rural communities where color had made so much difference in their lives. It still made a tremendous difference in this, the most notoriously ghettoized of American communities. They were employed as domestics or at less than skilled labor, nearly all 20 of these church women.

This evening they had been brought together in a workshop and, although most held jobs and had heavy family responsibilities, each in desperate search gave tentative commitment to the training schedule of eight sessions.

Most of the ex-Southerners had left their home towns some fifteen or more years ago to escape the "miseries of the 'turribl' South, hoping to find the Promised Land somewhere in this rich country." For them, however, Harlem was soon to prove a booby-trap, economically, socially, politically, psychologically. The excitement and awe of the big city early turned to disenchantment and despair, grime and filth, grind and drudgery—worse, to loneliness, anomia, and overwhelming nostalgia for the security and even the plodding pace of the South; to heartsick longing for friends and home folks who really cared. Disadvantaged and exploited by more sophisticated city old-timers, they were unwilling or unable to write loved ones of their dilemma. Soon were they to sink into the faceless anonymity of Harlem's suffering thousands, to come seeking solace, deliverance, and fellowship in the church.

But there was little of meaningful fellowship, even at the church, for such as they. For here as well, most of them were lost and lonely among the thousands with whom they worshipped. Isolated by their own anxieties and unwillingness to risk exposure of their naïveté and lack of urban know-what and know-how, they were to feel, because of limited schooling, uncertain economic or social status, their rural background, or darker skin tone, the rejection (imagined or real) by "those church big shots who couldn't even 'pass' themselves."

All this, these women who had awaited the opening session in small quiet desperate huddles, were able to share and confirm in depth of feeling, with each other. Within twenty minutes of the first conversation, one woman could say to the group, "In the seventeen years I was here, I never did tell nobody else except my very good friends that I came from Mississippi. I was warned never to say this or I'd never make my way."

When they found they had grown up in various pockets of the black South, so great was their hunger to make up time with each other, they could not contain the memories that came tumbling, gushing out. Happy ones, sad ones, beautiful ones, bitter ones, jostled for a chance to be told and shared. It did not seem to matter what the area of activity or life, they were replete with experiences and stories that set the group almost rolling off their chairs in gleeful remembering or wiping their eyes in tearful reminiscence.

The vivid word-pictures, for example, of a childhood spent dragging a yards-long bag between sun-scorched cotton rows and gathering endlessly the white fluffs which "came open all over the fields again the next morning, no matter how late you worked into the night getting every last one of the furry things," gave truth to some of the present-day derogatory intensity among Northern Negroes in the demand to "git your cotton-pickin' hands off." Once, while sharing delectable mouth-watering memories of the kitchen dining boards, they found themselves inadvertently lured into the "twist" on the off-beat of *Shortnin' Bread*. Their Baptist propriety took hold for one sheepish second, as they looked askance at each other, but did not stop them from going swingingly into a second chorus, which ended in an outburst of laugh-filled confessions of teenage escapades. Several adolescent daughters and granddaughters of members were present at this session; the inter-generation exchange was significant.

Here was a workshop which was made up, for the most part, not only of untrained leaders, but of women who had been deprived of any position of leverage in their church—in the words of a professional staff member, either "because of their own insecurity or because they had been pushed aside by more sophisticated leaders with an exaggerated idea of their own eminence."

Because of their lack of experience or their unfamiliarity with either the language or the principles of group dynamics, the training approach had to be modified. Their lack of intimacy with group constructs, however, meant also that they were not inhibited by or preoccupied with them. This could often be, and for these women may have been, their great strength. With guidance, they were able, in teams of two, to lead the group, beginning with the third session. Without advantage or disadvantage of technical jargon, they took over with minimal self-consciousness or timidity. They needed but to draw from the validity and depth of their own life experiences and the integrity of their simple and abiding faith in "our Savior and our Redeemer." One woman, for example, who needed to inquire whether chapter four and page four in the textbook were the same, led a session on memories of work which ended in a most significant sharing of commitment in God's service.

This was a group of women who appeared to have caught a glimpse of reality beyond the wearisome, dissipative incalcitrance of their day-to-day world. With third-ear sensibility, they had developed an attitude of awesome listening, and they could hear the voice of their God. For some it was a loud external voice, perhaps stern; for others, a quieter one, inside. Which, it did not matter. What was important was their capacity for inward perceiving; and, for most, for renewing, reassuring, transforming conversation with the Unseen.

In a setting where this kind of exchange was not only socially acceptable, but eagerly received, these women came together with their rejected past again; in a sense, with their rejected selves. The reunion was mirthful, poignant, joyous, healing. Hurtful experiences became integrated with high moments of religious illumination and commitment. They spoke with each other of the transcendence in simple words of such intense affect, immediacy, and conviction, culling insights of such clarity and wisdom as would make a theologian or psychiatrist gasp. A fresh sense of each, her own person, and the miracle and sacredness of its unique entity could best be measured in the healthful and genuine laughter that replaced the earlier embarrassed giggling, and the cleansing tears that washed off the anguished self-effacing, but not unresentful apologies which used to preface much of their recounting. Laughter and tears, feelings and ideas, came to ready confluence and were shared by each person with the authority of her particular constellation of experienced events, and the power to do so was exhilarating.

In the last of the training sessions, the admonition among participants (they had been sharing their own early school experiences and exchanging views on problems and inequities of educational opportunity for their children) was "Harlem is our South now. We must work for civil rights in the Black Belt at our backyard. We must start right here at our church."

That, indeed, they have begun doing. Already they have assigned to themselves the task of making welcome the more than 50 persons who come into their church membership each quarter. They plan a series of Group Conversations for each new group to insure increased church membership. One staff member reports further that they participate eagerly now in interracial functions, and that these are on the increase in the church. They have begun a drive to get voters to the polls. "They seem to have such a sense of their own worth, they are not afraid to give of themselves. We are amazed at how much they have grown in such a short time."

A Volunteer Organization Devoted to Open Housing

The Morris County Fair Housing Council in New Jersey has, since 1965, carried out the function of making it possible for anyone, regardless of race, creed, or national origin, to obtain suitable housing without discrimination. Recently, their constitution was amended to preclude economic discrimination as well, for, "our members became painfully aware that there can be no fair housing where there is no housing at all."

Being on the alert for all helpful approaches to achieving a community which prepares its children for life in an interracial world, some of the active members reached for Group Conversation.

A list of standing committees will give insight into the channels of service attempted by the Council: Housing Opportunities, the "field" committee which does the actual work of assisting the minority group home seeker; Low/Moderate Income Housing, which seeks to promote the development of moderately-priced housing of all sorts throughout the county; Public Relations; Education, which through its ongoing services to schools, churches and community organizations has reached 18,000 persons in 42 communities with the story of open housing; Membership, which sponsors "coffees" for new and potential members; Program, which seeks to continue the education of Council members through dialogue and forum programs; a monthly newsletter, *Open Letter,* circulated to members and friends around the county.

Because of the influx of industry into the area, the migration of peoples from urban centers and the growing pressures for equal employment opportunities, the county is bulging with home-seeking individuals from many regions of the world and from diverse family backgrounds.

Group Conversation is one method now being used by the Council for small, informal meetings which make up "Project Ripple," named by a whimsical member who was told by her neighbors not to make waves.

Project Ripple, as developed by the Education Committee of the Morris County Fair Housing Council, involves the invitation of uncommitted persons to meet in private homes in an effort to break down prejudices and acquaint people with the work of the Council. These sessions appear to be effective because people are more willing to ask honest questions and discuss what is really bothering them in small groups than in large, formal meetings. Each leader and co-leader is equipped with a list of goals, excerpted here.

To discussion leaders: What do we hope to achieve with these discussions, given the short time available? Our "awareness" goals—

1. *Awareness* that Morris County has classic, segregated housing patterns.

2. *Awareness* of the limitations this places on the quality of life lived in the suburbs (i.e. lack of meaningful contact with different kinds of persons; lack of challenge and openness in examining existing values; guilt in leading "the good life" at the expense of others;

development of a defensive, protective, "do-for-our-own-first" attitude toward planning, problem-solving, etc.)

3. *Awareness* of the limitations placed on education in white
suburbia. . . . If education is viewed as a preparation for life, what
preparation is offered by 18 years on the "Anglo-Saxon treadmill,"
(from home to school to scouts to church without much/any contact with anyone different racially, religiously or economically)?

4. *Awareness* that surrounding our towns and cities with closed,
unattainable suburbs removes incentives, breeds militancy and
creates slums.

5. *Awareness* that all of the measures taken to "protect" the
suburbs are self-defeating; the child forced to grow up in crowded,
substandard housing and receive a cut-rate education will grow
into the nonproductive adult, who will drain the taxpayer far more
than the cost today of urban-suburban shared responsibility.

6. *Awareness* that reaching half a dozen interested persons may
accomplish more than lecturing a huge but apathetic audience.

The Council, in its grassroots efforts to develop an awareness of
community problems in as diverse a cross-section of the populace
as possible, and to assist in translating that awareness into effective
problem-solving action, finds Group Conversation a welcome and
useful tool.

A hint of the change and growth implicit in the Council planning,
elements without which no organization can hope to remain a vital
force in the community it serves, may be found in a report of a past
president to the membership:

> Since our first president presented us with the challenge of in-
> cluding all segments of our population in our efforts, our think-
> ing has gradually modified; first came our own efforts to build
> moderate-income housing; then came our education to the fact
> that building codes and zoning ordinances effectively bar those
> of lower incomes from our communities; and finally came our
> realization that this situation is not healthy. We have changed
> enough so that at the present time we recognize the estrange-
> ment between the "haves" and the "have-nots" of both races.
> We realize there are some who do not wish to leave the ghetto
> and that our role should include two-way communication and
> assistance in solving the day-to-day problems of ghetto living.
> This does not mean that we have turned our backs on middle-
> class problems, only that our vision has broadened.

In line with this new vision of shared responsibility, a specially-funded program, called "Project Transition," has been put into effect by the Council. It employs a full-time, professional project director who contacts segments of the population most in need of recourse to public and/or private services; acts as a liaison with the power structure and aids potential home seekers in making an educated decision regarding whether to stay within the black community situation, or to make the move to integrated suburban life. Again, as with other facets of Council activity, Group Conversation helps to make the bridge-building to the wider community more feasible.

Moving a Senior Citizens Group

Bureaucratic red tape, snags in the system and new programs which no one understood, least of all the staff implementing the programs, made it impossible for individual older people to maintain a satisfactory relationship with the Department of Social Services without the help of the agency's project and social work staff. Panic and fear were growing among the senior citizens; and frustration among the staff, because of inability to make any sense out of the horrible conditions, was at the breaking point. There appeared to be only one way to insure that older people received the services and money they needed to maintain a decent standard of living—to become involved in social action and to demand an end to the confusion!

The members of the Hudson Guild–Fulton Senior Citizens Center had previously involved themselves in social action projects in a very minor way. Finally, an issue and two fortunate happenings occurred which launched a year of real involvement and growth.

The issue was the state cutbacks in welfare and Medicaid. One happening was a city-wide meeting of older people co-sponsored by the Community Council of Greater New York, the Department of Social Services, Division of Day Centers for Older People, and the National Council of Senior Citizens.

The speaker related to the older people by talking about their involvement in the development of unions, their very valid reasons for not being "well-off" now, and their responsibility to make this a better world for themselves and future generations of older people. Perhaps most important, he gave them the job of telling everyone at their centers of the need to protest the cutbacks. Six handpicked delegates did just that! Suddenly the group grew to include 25 people!

The second happening of particular significance to the project director was a training session for non-group workers in Group Conversation. The session was sponsored by the New York Friends Center Workshop. The group grew to 50 and with leadership became more creative than we had imagined possible.

The group continued to meet once a month, usually starting with Group Conversation, to talk about subjects important to them. They talked about what to do after the demonstration in Albany; what it is like living in retirement; what it means to be on welfare; and what role older people can play in social action. They began "conversations" with legislators to discuss what was happening, how they could be helpful to the legislators and what they could do.

During the year, ten action programs were supported by and reported to the membership, ranging from the first of a series of conversations with a state senator to delivering testimony to a Select Committee on Nutrition and Human Needs in the nation's capital.

One observation made: "Never use the first, second, or third answers which come to mind; stop and think of a fourth, fifth, and sixth answer to a problem."

Among the basic rules found operating, the key one is that age is not a common bond, and older people will rarely come together on an issue because of age. Other issues must be found which will draw older people together.

The project director, who had no training in group work, found Group Conversation so adequate for motivating individual participation that she used it at the start of a workshop for professional home economists, the goal of which was to help them understand how low-income families react to credit and money management. The Group Conversation experience enabled the home economists to clarify their own feelings about low-income families and to understand how their own cultural background and personal experience with money influenced their teaching of credit and money management. They could see that teaching "Family Planning and Spending to Reach Family Goals" is more than something in the textbooks, and that perhaps teachers have something to learn from those who have faced life on a different level.

7

Applications to Varied Settings

IT SHOULD BE clear that although there is a small amount of structuring in the group process described in these pages, that structuring must be changed and adapted to some extent to every new situation. As in any art form, one must first master the basic skills of that form. So we urge the new users of Group Conversation to follow the patterns explained in Chapter 3 before adapting its use to other types of situations. A dedicated leader soon comes to see that Group Conversation can fit into and bring out the social potential in many sorts of situations. These may range from being able to spontaneously change a dull dinner party into a memorable social occasion, to finding a way to "pull out" the best in a seven-hour plane seatmate, or being able to start a Group Conversation when he, the leader, understands not a word of the language of the 18 participants in the circle. One might use three words to tell what saves the situation—inner security, humility and spontaneity.

"Spontaneous activity is the one way in which man can overcome the terror of the aloneness without sacrificing the integrity of the self, for in a spontaneous realization of the self man unites himself anew with the world. Love is the foremost component of such spontaneity because it leads to oneness and yet does not eliminate individuality." *

* Fromm, Erich, *Escape from Freedom*, (New York, Farrar & Rinehart, 1941).

113

But the ability to stimulate spontaneity rests within the personality of the leader. Only his own basic and ever-growing sense of security within himself (to seek this must be a never-ending life work for each of us) will enable him to try out new ways and not be upset if puzzling situations develop, or at worst if some individual, because of his own insecurity, lashes out at the leader in an open-ended social situation. This does not often happen but at any time it might. If one does not love the maimed and the halt as he does the well and the attractive, one should not be a group leader. Therefore, in a "ticklish" situation he reaches out and figuratively embraces the lasher. And yet, since the main aim of Group Conversation is not group therapy but is to help the participants achieve a healthy sense of oneness, the leader must be firm in not allowing the illness of one to destroy the sense of groupness for the others. In such situations the leader relies on the help of his co-leader not only during the situation but afterwards in giving him constructive and sincere criticism. There is no formula for stopping the too-long talker, or the bitter person who lashes out; one simply relies on the power of love and one's intuition.

In this chapter the reports show how varied are the settings in which the flexible use of Group Conversation has been of value. Whether the group was made up of physically and intellectually deprived Southern rural Negroes receiving, in groups, government food stamps; college upperclassmen finding ways to welcome and integrate freshmen into campus life, or small groups of Quakers in eight European countries speaking a different language than the leader—always the spontaneity based on love released in the group, made for each participant a memorable and growth-engendering experience.

Teaching Nutrition Facts to Food Stamp Recipients

AUSPICES: Southern Rural Action, Inc., for the Taliaferro County, Georgia, Emergency Food Stamp Project.

GOALS: To use Group Conversation to teach nutritional skills in a food stamp program aimed at improving the participants' health, and help the project staff better understand the underlying causes of poor food habits. (Tapes, including video, were made of all sessions to assist subsequent evaluation.)

SITUATION: A medical report had revealed that food stamp recipients of all ages had extreme hypertension, lacked sufficient iron and calcium, had low intake of carotene (found in green and yellow vegetables), and had a high incidence of heart abnormalities.

SESSION ONE.

TOPIC: Food Memories Around the Meal to Be Discussed Today.

LEAD QUESTIONS (designed to elicit childhood memories of, for example, breakfast; of food habits.and family customs):

1. Where did we grow up? How many children were there in our family?

2. What sounds woke us up in the morning? What breakfast smells? Was it mostly the same kind of food each morning?

3. Did our family eat together at this meal? If not, when?

4. What special meals did our family regularly have? Did the special meals give us a sense of closeness to our family? What special foods did we have at those special meals? Were there special activities around the table—Bible reading? prayers? songs?

5. Besides feelings of family closeness, did we feel resentments? Who was the boss in the family? Who punished us? How did we feel about all this as children?

6. What childhood illnesses do we remember? Did we have a regular family doctor? Did older people who knew herbs or patent medicines serve our families during illnesses?

7. Describe our leaving the home to go to school each morning. Was it a time of family conflict and tension, or cooperation and calmness? What kind of lunch did we like to take to school? Did we ever buy lunch at school? at a nearby store?

8. When we married and had a home of our own, what changes did we make in our food habits? Give a word picture of you and your husband getting up and having breakfast. What dishes do we make when we want to please our husband or children when they come home? Do we see well-prepared food as a way of expressing our love?

9. What changes in our food habits do we in this county need to make today because of the changes in the way we live—having frozen foods and refrigerators and new scientific discoveries in nutrition, as well as doing the kinds of work which burn fewer calories?

CLOSING: Discussion led by nutritionist on changes in food habits needed in today's world.

SESSION TWO.

TOPIC: Food for Young Mothers and Their Babies; Early Superstitions about Pregnancy and Childbirth.

LEAD QUESTIONS (source ideas):

1. "Old wives" tales; superstitions about specific foods' effects on unborn child, on mother, on birth, etc.

2. Patterns for naming the baby: family names, biblical names; ceremonies for dedication of the child to the good life, or to the service of God (story of Hannah and Samuel from the Old Testament).

3. Value of singing favorite lullabies to, playing with, and lovingly touching the infant.

CLOSING: Provided a bridge for the nutritionist to give the group clearly and simply the facts on the close relationship between the pregnant mother's diet and the unborn child's brain development and the child's later I.Q., as well as the effects on mind and body of the child's diet from birth on.

SESSION THREE.

TOPICS: Teenagers and Food; How to Use Food to Bring More Joy into Life. (Because teenagers can influence their parents in changing family food habits, this Group Conversation involved parents with their teenagers.)

LEAD QUESTIONS (source ideas):

1. Compare the foods we had at parties: the parents—ginger cake, chocolate fudge and molasses candy (for pulling), all of which was probably homemade; the teenagers—potato chips, "Coke" with ice cream—all of which are bought today, but the fun is just the same.

2. "We are what we eat!" Eat well to feel alive!

CLOSING:

1. Ideas were shared for having more fun around foods in our homes as well as at parties. Other ideas exchanged: have more special meals (not necessarily to cost any more) just to "celebrate each other's existence"; special meals to celebrate birthdays, special honors, school graduation, holidays, new jobs, the change in the seasons—even the first strawberry or radish in our gardens.

2. The nutritionist discussed the high cost of the "empty calorie" in things like "soda pop," candies, etc., which are low in nutritional value. Spending our money on such items leaves less for foods rich in nutrients.

RESULTS OF THE THREE SESSIONS: Follow-up through observation, interviews, and playing back the tapes of fourteen hours of Group Conversation showed significant changes in food habits of the participating families. Grocery store owners in the town reported the purchase of more oranges, fruit juices, liver and red meats, fresh vegetables and dry milk, and less lard and fatty meats. More people, especially the high school youth, were now eating nutritious breakfasts.

Helping School and Home Work Together *

In a New York City tension area, the local Parents Association had almost ceased to function because of intergroup prejudices. We will briefly describe the four-year program which was developed and which reactivated the Association and overcame much of the tension in the school and the neighborhood.

The initial step was to be the involvement and the training of a small group of concerned mothers and teachers.

This first small group of potential leaders was of mixed religious, racial and national backgrounds. The Puerto Rican mother could scarcely speak English, but the atmosphere of acceptance and trust created by the group's first Group Conversation gave her courage. Though she was obviously nervous, she was able to say: "We need this badly. We Puerto Ricans are not welcome around here. Even you teachers," and she looked straight at one, "what you call it?" Here she vigorously moved her elbows. Someone in the group gave the American term "push around." By this time, the tears were streaming down her face, and sympathetically down the faces of almost everyone, for we knew the truth of her accusations, and she knew that we knew.

These mothers after the training, led Group Conversations in their own homes. Other mothers were invited to each of the seven

* From a detailed report in *Neighbors in Action,* Rachel Davis DuBois (New York, Harper and Row, 1950).

homes, over a period of seven weeks, making 49 home groups, with about 15 participants in each.

During this time, friendly contacts were made with 295 mothers, one-third of whom were Puerto Rican Americans never before reached by the school. Many became members of the Parents Association. A committee on intercultural education was added, with representatives from eight different ethnic groups to help make and carry out decisions in regard to the developing program.

Parranda from Puerto Rico. When a Puerto Rican mother told vividly of her memories of *parrandas,* the leader's eyes traveled in memory over the apartment houses in the school's neighborhood, the steep walk-ups, with doors of every apartment locked against their neighbors. "Don't you think we could try a *parranda* here? We don't know each other enough." Faces lighted and heads nodded hopefully. And so it was that a culture pattern of a low-status group came not only to be esteemed by the whole gathering, but adopted by both the Parents Association and the school faculty as a working program.

We can give here only a short outline of the *parranda* program,* during the four years it was conducted as a regular school activity. The one *parranda* a week, organized by the growing numbers of devoted and committed members of the Parents Association (two homes, "the main-dish" and "the dessert" hostesses, of different cultural backgrounds were visited on school time, from twelve to three o'clock during the school year, for four years), was participated in by 14 pupils—two selected from each of the seven sections of the seventh-grade social studies classes. The project fitted perfectly into one of the study units of this grade, "American Home Life." The mothers or other members of the families of the 14 pupils were also invited. Thus, the child and parent had an emotionally-satisfying experience at the same time.

The *parranda* experience was an adaptation of Group Conversation led by mothers who had been members of the first training group. The subject matter focused on "How American Families Work, Play, Love and Worship." Each *parranda* experience was reported weekly to the social studies classes by the pupils who had

---

* Almost every culture has progressive parties. We used the word "parranda" because it came from a Spanish-speaking mother and because that group at that time was in need of being recognized as having something valuable to contribute to others.

participated in that week's *parranda*. The teachers used these reports of experiences in homes of various backgrounds to develop
their "experience-centered curriculum" consisting of various kinds
of classroom units.

A Report of a Typical Parranda

We were a representative group of Americans, as we started
out from the school for the first home: Jewish Americans,
Catholic Americans, Protestant Americans, a Mormon, a
Quaker, Negroes, Puerto Ricans. Recent comers were represented by a lad from Belgium, and a little girl from Caracas,
while the older immigration had come from Vienna, Russia,
Poland. Other regions of this country were represented—the
West by Idaho, the North by Minnesota, the East by Pennsyl-
vania and New Jersey, and of course, New York State.

When the formalities of the introductions had been con-
cluded, and the leader told the hostess (a Daughter of the
American Revolution, old-stock American) the purpose of
our visit, she began: "I grew up on a farm in North Dakota,
and we all worked together. There was much to do: preparation of the meals for the men who came to help with the plow-
ing in the spring; later on, for the threshing crews, and for
those picking the fruit in the fall. But then work was a virtue
the early Americans had to possess, in order to build this
great country of ours."

Another old-stock American said: "I too, grew up on a
farm. We used to work all day, and then go to the Grange at
night and sing about it. Does anyone remember the song
'Work for the Night Is Coming'?" It seemed that several of
the oldsters did, for they joined her in singing it.

The youngsters were brought easily into the Group Conversation. "How does the way work is done now differ from
the way it used to be done?" A little five-year-old sister of
one of the pupils said: "A long time ago, they used the broom,
but now we use vacuum cleaners," and then tried to hide behind the person next to her because, with all eyes upon her,
she found herself momentarily embarrassed. "Yes," someone
took up the theme, "do you recall how we used to beat rugs
on the line? Life is easier now."

Another oldster, a grandmother of one of the pupils, gave

a vivid description of a Vermont sugaring-off party, the buckets hanging on the trees to be emptied and re-emptied by men wearing fur mittens, for it is freezing when the sap is ready to be tapped. And then the fun of putting the boiled sap on snow, to eat like delicious candy. The hostess then served maple sugar candy, as a traditional American confection.

The children told easily of their work at home: washing dishes with mother or sister—boys as well as girls—making beds, running errands, being responsible for the thorough cleaning of their rooms on Saturday.

"But life, even in the old days, was not all given to work, was it?" asked the leader.

"No, indeed, we had parties, strawberry festivals and dances, though we sometimes combined work with a party, like a house-raising or helping a neighbor cut up fruit before drying it."

"Oh, yes, there is a song about 'Aunt Dinah's Quilting Party' which was used long ago as an opportunity for lovers to meet. Do you remember? 'It was from Aunt Dinah's Quilting Party I was seeing Nellie home'." The children had learned it in school and had fun singing it with the older folks.

"How did courting in the old days compare with courting customs now?" asked the leader keeping in mind the four categories of her topic—Work, Play, Love and Worship.

Before more than a mention of "The Surrey with the Fringe on Top" could be made, it was time to move on to the next home. Of course, our hostess and the grandmother went with us for *parrandas* grow in number of participants as they go along. This was an Irish-American home.

The grandparents were born in Ireland, and talked interestingly of the music of the war-pipes, which they illustrated by playing a record, pointing out the difference between it and the music of the Scottish bagpipes; the art of storytelling, a traditional practice of that group, was illustrated by the eight-year-old granddaughter who recited an Irish fairy tale. She regularly performed over the radio on Sunday. The grandfather, a Gaelic scholar, compared that language with Basque, and then recited a poem for us, which caused one of the youngsters to say: "Oh, that sounds something like Hebrew."

Whereupon, he was asked to recite something in Hebrew, which he did.

We were then escorted to the dining-room for tea and "trifle," a kind of cottage pudding which is a traditional dish in this Irish-American family.

For the next eight weeks, until the end of that school year, and for three years thereafter, one *parranda* a week was conducted in the following kinds of American home: Italian, Jewish, Puerto Rican, Irish, old-line Protestant, Chinese, German and Czech. These trips covered two homes during the school day, from noon to three p.m. The following autumn and for three more years, the *parranda* program became an integral part of the program of the school and the Parents Association. Emphasis was on training volunteer leaders and on follow-up in school and home.

Follow-up in the Parents Association: During these four years, most of the activities of the Parents Association grew out of some phase of the project. For example, Group Conversation was used (1) as a means of more quickly channeling to the mothers information on the health resources and responsibilities of the city's Health Department, and (2) to inspire young parents to start a study group in early childhood education.

At one point mothers from eight different culture groups started a seminar on home customs and became their own cultural informants. Students from the Family Life Department of nearby Columbia's Teachers College came regularly to give some volunteer leadership while learning at firsthand about school-community problems.

Follow-up in the school: The *parranda* program helped to answer several needs. It fitted into the seventh-grade syllabus on "American Home Life." It helped fill some of the emotional and social needs of Junior High School pupils. It helped, by the emphasis on cross-cultural exchange, to enrich the family life of all participants.

The school procedure: One teacher was appointed each semester to work closely with the Parents Association Committee in charge of *parrandas*. These teachers sent records of *parranda* conversations to each seventh-grade teacher, as well as to the principal and the committee of the Parents-Association. This enabled the teacher the better to conduct the follow-up classroom discussion and relate it to the syllabus.

Faculty conferences: These made it possible for teachers to share with one another whatever activity units they were developing out of the *parranda* experience and to coordinate around these other school activities such as assembly programs, field trips and extra-curricular club activities. Titles of some of these activity units were: "Folklore from Far and Near," "Food Facts and Fancies," "Sing a Song," "Home Customs Around the Calendar." *

In the community: Parrandas sometimes ended in the public library with Puerto Rican, Irish and other American culture group storytellers as guests of honor. Two churches asked for and received names of pupils who had taken leadership roles in the *parranda* program. These pupils gave similar leadership in their Sunday schools.

The school and some of the community organizations cooperated at the end of each school year in an all-school community festival entitled, "Neighbors At Work and Play." In the gymnasium, the folklore, songs and dances collected and learned during the year were exhibited. Parents and children participated together in their presentation.

Training and giving guidance to new leaders. In our public schools parents come and go as they follow their children up the grades. So, new mothers had to be trained and guided to lead a *parranda* which is Group Conversation adapted to the informality and frequent interruptions that are natural in a situation when a group of people visit a hostess and are served food as a part of the hospitality. Expecting such interruptions, the leader held in mind the following areas of conversation which went on as informally and spontaneously as possible and yet with some assurance that it was a learning, intercultural experience. Not all of these topics would be touched on in a single session.

1. Each person gives name and place of birth and place of birth of parents. (Leader stresses fact that we are all Americans.)

2. Bring in *different ways of greeting people,* such as the French custom of kissing each cheek or the touching of noses by the Maoris of New Zealand, and the ways of other cultures. Bring in the different kinds of shelter. All people have homes. What are they

* For copies of these unpublished units, send to New York Friends Center, 15 Rutherford Place, New York, N.Y. 10003 (25¢ each).

called? Igloo, wigwam, bungalow, chateau, apartment, house, palace, etc. Suggested songs: "Home Sweet Home" or "Home on the Range," or similar songs in other languages.

3. *Food Served:* Bring in the different patterns of hospitality of different groups such as the meaning of bread and salt, carrying a candle to a home where the people have just moved in. When the food is being served is an excellent time to talk about "graces." Suggest that many families say grace before meals, a few say it at the end—the Norwegians, for instance. Ask children and adults who happen to know a grace, to repeat it. See in how many languages a grace is known. Perhaps someone can sing a grace. If candles are used on the table or in the room, the conversation may be directed to the use of candles to lend a festive atmosphere and from that to the specific use of candles for various occasions.

4. *Holidays, Red Letter Days:* This might include Hallowe'en, Thanksgiving, Purim, Carnival in Puerto Rico, Chinese New Year with its dragon parade or Mardi Gras. Allow for spontaneous expression of appropriate songs, dances and singing games.

5. *Exchanging of gifts* will lead from masks and costumes and the custom of asking for pennies at Hallowe'en, now expressed in the United Nations Children Program "Trick or Treat," Thanksgiving and Purim to gift-giving at Christmas, Chanukah, Easter, birthdays, confirmation and graduation.

Welcoming Freshmen to a College Campus

During freshman orientation week the new students at a midwestern college found themselves in groups of 15 for three sessions of dialogue with teams of upperclassmen. The previous weekend these 40 upperclassmen, working as leaders and co-leaders, were asked to learn the technique of Group Conversation and to develop three topics to fit their needs. They evolved the following:

Who Am I? The Meaning of Being an Individual.

The Meaning of Community Living.

The Implications of a Liberal Education.

The chief warning given the leaders was to steer participants away from intellectualizing by holding them to sharing their experiences. Each session went into a discussion of how the participants see themselves today and on this college campus (Earlham).

* * *

SESSION ONE.

TOPIC: *Who Am I? The Meaning of Being an Individual.*

PLACING: Give name and various places where we have lived. "There is no one in the world like you, never was, and never will be. It is your excuse for being."—Frank Harris.

LEAD QUESTIONS:

Before asking how well am I going to do in college, let's try to see ourselves as an emerging personality in family or neighborhood.

1. At the age of ten, did we have a pet? a collection—records? books?

2. What recognition did we have from others—favorable? unfavorable? Were we defensive, protective of our property? How did we express it? How did we compensate for failure to win approval?

3. What activities did the community give us for a feeling of success? Does anyone remember being laughed at? Who helped us most at that stage? Who was the most frightening?

4. Is it easier to do what other people think we should do? If we have a sense of "what I must be," do we know how we got it?

5. What are some means to personal awareness of a pattern of growth which we may have—dreams? role-playing? Does this quotation have meaning for us: "We are responsible for other people's ability to be themselves"?

During the weekend training workshop the upperclass trainees had been led in a Group Conversation on the topic, "Who Am I?" This was followed by a card response to the question, "What is it to be an individual?" Among their responses to the question, "What presented an obstacle to you during your freshman year?" they recalled: anxieties (one was relationship with other black students *), overemphasis on intellectualism, soul-searching, too many planned activities, fear of nonacceptance due to racial background, lack of self-confidence, lack of money, being stereotyped as a roughneck athlete, uncertainty of relationships, and personal items such as adaptation to a more open-minded society in regard to war and social conditions. These responses were made available to each team as they prepared themselves to lead the new students on the same topic. Being reminded of how involved they had been as they

---

* For the seriousness of this problem in some colleges today see *New York Times Magazine,* Jan. 18, 1970, "Two Nations at Wesleyan University" by Richard J. Margolis.

recorded their freshman experiences helped them to identify with the newcomers in their problems of adjustment in a new college year.

SESSION TWO.
TOPIC: *Living in a College Community.*
PLACING: As we were growing up, how many were at home for us to get along with?
LEAD QUESTIONS:
1. What were the games we played when adults were not present? Who decided what to play? What happened when things went wrong?
2. Do we remember breaking a rule at home or school or "gang" and being punished? Did we feel it was justified?
3. What were some of the rules in high school which we followed or broke?
4. Who recalls a difficult situation which we accepted because it was fair?
DISCUSSION (high school and college "rules and regulations" as reported by leaders):
"High school dress codes, responsibility for petty rules were real concerns in my group. They talked to each other; there was a relaxed atmosphere and laughing."
"We reached no conclusions, yet we were all better aware of the dichotomy which exists between an individual and the society he is a part of."
"I left with the feeling that I knew these kids, and they, me, on a special level—more honest and open. I could share with them my fears and joys, and I was able to experience their emotions. Among the factors for this openness was the spontaneity."
"In my group the rapport was good enough to go quite honestly into rules and regulations. About halfway through the ninety minutes I brought up specific campus issues, such as drugs, alcohol, hours, etc. They liked the experience and wanted more discussion during the rest of the year."
"Talking about one's childhood and bringing up humor are good ways to relax and open up."

SESSION THREE.
TOPIC: *The Implications of a Liberal Education.*

PLACING: Give nickname and type of elementary school setting: urban, rural, etc.

LEAD QUESTIONS:

1. Who can give a brief description of the room of our favorite grade teacher?

2. Who or what taught us something we were really excited about?

3. Were we ever punished in school? What did we learn from it?

4. Do we recall a person who got us on a trail of our own interest? Did a "gang" form around this interest?

5. In what field of study is our present preference? Are there problems related to this?

6. How do we react toward new situations and persons? Do we have an experience of changing our feeling about a situation or person?

7. In high school, who was our favorite poet or philosopher? Can we recall any of his words of wisdom?

DISCUSSION (as reported by leaders):

". . . at the end we shifted into a discussion of political ideology and had a level-headed discussion of the problems of self-compromise for pragmatic solutions. My ending was just to point out that we had had a good example of standing up for oneself and also respecting the other guy."

"My group intellectualized too much. I guess it was to keep from having to deal on the more personal, experiential level. They are used to dealing with ideas, and thus ideas are less threatening."

EVALUATIONS:

In this situation a panel discussion for the whole student body on "What Is a Liberal Education" had preceded the series of Group Conversations. The panelists were professors and upperclassmen. Those who were leaders in the Group Conversations on the same subject felt that it might have been better to have had the panel follow the Group Conversations. Also: "It would help if the professors talked in a more personal way about what a liberal education means to them."

The final word in evaluations was to the effect that "we feel these groups did provide worthwhile experiences and a needed variety in freshman activities." The desirability of using other group patterns was also expressed.

Lead Questions for Worker–Employer Situations *

Aim: To develop mutual understanding between "poverty-affected youth" and those who work with them on the job, both bosses and co-workers. *Leaders* should be those of good experience, who through associations can empathize with the participants.

LEAD QUESTIONS:

1. What does a good job well done feel like—in our bodies (hands, back muscles, etc.)? Can one put into words the feeling of physical tiredness?

2. What does working with others feel like? Is there a different *feeling* when we have to work alone and when we work with others? Give experiences.

3. Do we have different feelings working on jobs where we are bossed by a foreman who seems to dislike us?

4. Interaction on equal grounds—with fellow workers, with bosses: when does this happen—on the job? at coffee break? when eating lunch?

5. Were we ever a boss or the leader of a group—responsible that all those under us would do a certain thing well or in a particular way and at a particular time and place?

6. To what kinds of work can we give "our all"? What feelings did our ancestors have when they built this country—its railroads, skyscrapers, etc.? Do we in any way share similar feelings in our work?

7. What kind of pioneering do we Americans have to try to do today? Black Power? "white power"? "shared power"?

One's Religious Faith—A Three–Session Dialogue

Quaker Dialogue has been used with some four hundred small groups of members of the Religious Society of Friends in all parts of the United States, in Mexico City, several cities in Canada, and in eight European countries in multi-translation. This report is not offered to convert strangers to Quakerism but to help produce among members and attenders of Friends' Meetings and other spir-

* This topic has had very careful planning with several individuals representing both employer and worker. The actual leading of a group conversation in such a setting is pending as this book goes to print.

itually-motivated groups a sense of renewal within themselves and in their faith. Readers who desire to know more about the Religious Society of Friends are referred to the bibliography at the end of this book.

The Quaker Dialogue, then, is directed toward making it possible for the participants of the group to share informally and spontaneously their experiences, ideas and concerns toward the goal of spiritual renewal within themselves and of releasing more creative energy for spreading God's kingdom. In three two-hour sessions which, with the same participants, follow each other closely, these topics are used:

1. Our religious experiences both outside and within the Meeting for Worship.

2. The nature and role of the Quaker method of "finding the sense" of the Business Meeting without taking a vote.

3. The responsibility of Friends to their social testimonies, i.e., peace, racial equality, and simplicity.

Lest the reader become confused with our use of terms, Quaker Dialogue uses the method of Group Conversation by evoking memories of early experiences related to the contents of each of the three two-hour sessions. The term "dialogue" covers the total process. Members of any faith as well as an interfaith group could get positive results by applying the principles of dialogue to the needs of their own group, i.e., the sharing of experiences in practicing their beliefs and using, during the process, a few brief, pertinent quotations from their religious leaders past and present.

The Dialogue leader's role is to help participants communicate with each other in an understanding way about areas of experience which deeply matter to them. When statements become abstract or academic, the leader asks for personal experiences related to the particular subject. Offering his own is helpful. No pressure for agreement or a group decision is allowed for it would inhibit frankness and spontaneity. The usual practices of many religious groups, such as the singing of hymns and vocal prayer, will be woven spontaneously into the Dialogue or perhaps at the ending.

The group members are asked to be constructively critical of the way they worship together, of the effectiveness of the decision-making processes within their church or temple, and of the personal and organizational responsibility toward social problems. Of course, arguments should be avoided. Creative suggestions from the Dialogue group are often channeled to the policy-making leaders of their church or temple.

SESSION ONE: The Meeting for Worship

> Quaker worship is a method for inducing the Light of God to flood into the conscious mind, a therapy and an occasion for praise, and sometimes, through grace, for the practice of His Presence . . . as with all methods it is open to failure for a hundred and one reasons . . . Because we are not alone, and are all concentrating to the one end, suddenly he [the participant] will notice the profound stillness and feel himself to be within it. Now perhaps someone may speak, others might follow in the same vein, and a group sermon develops . . . More intense stillness comes when perhaps the whole Meeting lifts its face in loving silence, and then the final silent or vocal thanks, and the Meeting breaks with the shaking of hands.*

Following the basic structure of Group Conversation, the leader, after the usual brief period of silent worship, introduces the aim and nature of the Dialogue (it is not discussion) and asks for a sharing of "our earliest religious experiences in the broad sense of the word." He has the participants place themselves as to where they grew up, recalling, if they can, a special spot in a house or near it where they liked to be (this last may be changed by a leader if he sees fit). He then moves to lead questions about, for example, our first prayers: "Were any of us brought up on 'Now I lay me down to sleep'?" The diversity of such experiences comes in a relaxed, informal, sometimes humorous way, such as, "My first prayer was very functional. I was treed by a bull for a whole afternoon." Those experiences lead naturally into the second category the leader has in mind, namely, the "minor ecstasy" ** (being taken out of ourselves in joy and wonderment), moments many children have, when they say: "I still remember how I felt when I first saw a bunch of white violets at the foot of an oak tree," or "Yes, and

* John Sykes, *The Quakers* (Philadelphia, J. B. Lippincott Co., 1959).
** See Elizabeth Gray Vining, *The World in Time* (New York, Harper and Bros., 1954).

I remember how I felt when at ten I first saw the birth of a lamb. I ran in to tell my mother." To give even deeper significance to these experiences, the leader may read a quotation from an adult mystical experience, such as one from O'Neill's *Long Day's Journey into Night:*

> Edmund talks to his father: "When I was on the Squarehead square rigger, bound for Buenos Aires. Full Moon in the Trades. The old hooker driving fourteen knots. I lay on the bowsprit, facing astern, with the water foaming into spume under me, the masts with every sail white in the moonlight, towering high above me. I became drunk with the beauty and singing rhythm of it, and for a moment I lost myself—actually lost my life. I was set free! I dissolved in the sea, became white sails and flying spray, became beauty and rhythm, became high dim-starred sky! I belonged, without past or future, with peace and unity and a wild joy, within something greater than my own life, or the life of man, to life itself. To God, if you want to put it that way.

This quotation (a leader can choose his own, of course) readily leads into the main category: "Does anything like this ever happen to us in a Meeting for Worship or any other religious service?" At this point, each leader will make his own list of lead questions according to which experiences of the participants need to be elicited, such as: Have we ever gone to Meeting very tired or feeling upset, and come away feeling rested and calm? What happens? Is it the Spirit seeking us as we seek the Spirit? When is our Meeting not at its best? What can happen to stop the flow of the Spirit? Our own resentments and anxieties? Can we share some of these now?

On several occasions, the anxieties shared in the Dialogue were expressed on three generational levels. *From the older participants:* "How can I make new friendships now that most of my loved ones have died?" *From the middle-aged:* "The kinds of responsibility I must carry in my family and work are sometimes most overwhelming." *From the youth:* "And I'm not sure there will even be a world for me to work and raise a family in." It was helpful at this point to quote Tom Kelly:

> Within us is a meeting place with God, who strengthens and invigorates our whole personality and makes us new creatures.

The tempests and inner strain of self-seeking, self-oriented living grow still. We learn to be worked through; serenity takes the place of anxiety.*

Each session of a Quaker Dialogue usually ends in fifteen or twenty minutes of meditative worship.

SESSION TWO

We need to suggest here only the lead questions most profitably used to carry a Quaker Dialogue group into the sharing of their experiences in their Business Meetings, and to emphasize the value of again taking the same group into childhood experiences. This time, the placing is developed around the participants' sibling relationships. Typical lead questions follow.

What were the games we played when adults did not direct them? How did we choose our leaders? By chance? taking turns? recognizing ability? other ways? How did we feel if we were not chosen until last? Our own behavioral insights and those of others come quickly in such give-and-take. (Once, in response to the question, "Did we play school?" several said, "Yes, yes!" With the next question, "Who was the teacher?" one participant replied, "Oh, I *always* was." "She still is," the group responded.) Who remembers a bully? Were we ever his victim? How did we feel?

What school experiences had we in using *Robert's Rules of Order?* When did we first experience and understand the reasons basic to the Quaker way of arriving at the sense of the Meeting without taking a vote? (Quite often this experience has been a great revelation. But for some Friends, especially those who do not understand it, the Business Meeting is often a boring, time-consuming experience. To enrich our understanding, we have often used this observation from Howard H. Brinton in *The Spiritual Message of the Society of Friends:*

Friends, accordingly, do not vote in making decisions as group, for, since there is only one Truth and this Truth is, in the long run, accessible to all, a patient search for it will eventually lead to unity. This means that each person in the group is present not to defend an opinion, but to join in a common search and a united finding. A group of scientists would not think of arriving at a scientific truth by voting. For

* From *Reality of the Spiritual World* (New York, Harper & Row).

the same reason, the Quakers do not believe that the truth of an opinion is dependent on the number of those who hold it.*

Assuming that the leaders and the Dialogue participants know the whys and wherefores of the Friends' method of "getting the sense of the meeting," the leader's role is to hold the group which meets regularly in its own Business Meeting to their actual experiences in those Meetings, but to do this in terms of basic reasons for *not* taking a vote.

Take, for example, the use of intuition: quite often it is found that Friends are not conscious of some of the basic processes they are using. If the sharing of actual experiences can bring vividly to the fore some of these processes, they are more likely to be used. For instance, few Friends realize the importance of giving heed to the intuitive process which some people possess more than others. One Meeting postponed an important decision for no other reason than that a Friend said, "I don't know why, but I feel very uneasy about this decision we are about to minute." By the time of the next Meeting, events had proved that the Friend's intuition was right.

Other reasons for not taking a vote: absorbing each other's values; going into the Silence to wait for openings; finding the creative way out; keeping the Spirit of Prayer during the whole Business Meeting. Sometimes in a Quaker Dialogue, the group will role-play an experience until they can see what could have been done during a recent difficult Business Meeting. And, finally, because people are human, the method of consensus sometimes just does not work!

Again, the closing is often a period of silent worship, with particular reference to the religious basis of the Business Meeting.

SESSION THREE

Usually in its third meeting the group is ready to go directly into a fruitful discussion. They are expected to choose their own topic. It may be one of their Quaker testimonies, or relate to some form of outreach. Typical of the latter are these questions on outreach, evolved by the New Swarthmore Community, a group of young people living as simply as possible in a commune at Clinton, N.Y.:

* Leaflet; available from Friends General Conference, 1520 Race Street, Philadelphia, Pa., 19002.

How can we share our light with others in a new and more effective way of spreading the Good News? How can we bring the power of the Lord to bear on a diseased and dangerous world?

A Venture in Intercultural Living

> For the first time I realized how middle-class my orientation was, and I didn't like what I felt and saw in myself. Since then, all summer, I have been tutoring children from a ghetto neighborhood to come into greater self-realization and dignity, to learn and maybe to love a person like myself. Other summers I had spent most weekends in the country.

What encounter brought about this feeling in one of the adult participants? It was a week in July 1968 which Powell House (a Quaker retreat and conference center) publicized as "An Intercultural Search for a Deeper Sense of Community in Our Homes and in Our Nation." Our aims in typical middle-class fashion were:

> to grow in friendship across cultural lines,
>
> to grow in appreciation of worthwhile differences,
>
> to grow in facing the many problems that beset us in our local communities and our nation.

Our differences were to be those of age, class, race and religion— the kind of differences whose walls separate human beings in most of America's neighborhoods.

July 7th, our opening date, found us driving up the Indian-named Taconic Parkway to lovely, quiet Old Chatham in the foothills of the Catskills. We included two Harlem families with two adults and eleven children ranging from two to eighteen; an American Indian family with four children ranging from three to ten; a Jewish family with two boys, twelve and fourteen, and an adopted daughter of mixed parentage; and a Puerto Rican family with two girls and a teenage boy. Already at Powell House was a Quaker family with two adopted children, one of whom is Indian, and their own son. And then there was a young mother with her first baby of seven months, the father a busy principal in a Brooklyn school. Add to these the several Powell House staff adults, plus five or six other adults eagerly looking forward to this experience of being with children as an added emotional attraction for their vacation, and you have high human potential.

During our first gathering Sunday evening we gave our names and birthdays. We could see that our ages made a time span from seven months to seventy years. We then divided ourselves into six family groups by dancing an adaptation of "The Farmer Takes a Wife," during which each man was to take a different woman for his "pretend" wife at the table for the week: Puerto Rican, Jewish, Quaker, Harlem, Indian, and mountaineer (we had a family from the mountains of Kentucky). These family groups were to sit at the same tables for the week, taking turns being responsible for the total group's participation in grace at meals, morning worship fellowships, the evening meal, and games in the early evening with adult discussion afterward.

It was fun and meaningful for all ages, this seven-day role-playing of the extended family. One of the men became the "father" of the children at the Indian table. "He'll never be the same again," said his wife. The little children took seriously their extended-family role-play and went to their "foster parents" for help or fun at any time or place. We experienced each other's culture and family atmosphere in a way we never can forget. "Being mother to the two Harlem boys, I could sense their alertness yet could see that their schooling had not given them equal opportunity to learn as had the ten-year-old of our Quaker family. I've read and heard of this before, but now I know it in my deepest feelings."

The Indian Family—Monday. Very vivid is the memory of the American Indian grace led by the mother as she gave thanks for food and light, standing with arms stretched high, and with all of us repeating her words. After the evening dinner there were Indian games on the lawn and then Indian dancing in the large common room. The mothers' anti-war dance in which only mothers could participate radiated something deep and symbolic.

The discussion after the children were put to bed took us into some problems which the Indians face today. "Yes, we are participating in the Poor People's Campaign, for there is much poverty among us, also." "We are not ready, yet, to leave the reservation, for we need the land; and one way to hold on to it is through our families." "One of our valuable customs is that of the extended family. A grandparent in a tribe is grandparent to all the children."

The Jewish Family—Tuesday. This was the day assigned for the Jewish family table to share with all of us their most cherished family meal, the Seder. Perhaps seven-month-old Kathie did not sense its significance, but everyone else from the two-year-old up caught it—the freedom holiday. We sang "Go Down, Moses" and the traditional Seder table songs. There was the traditional focus on children: four of the children each read one of the four questions which start this meal, and all ran to find the hidden Mazoth, without which the meal cannot be finished. Most of us could see the value of Christians and Jews at least once in a while joining in the Passover Meal which is the basis for the Christian communion —the last supper of Jesus, who, as a child, must have often found the Mazoth, and received his reward. One of the adults wrote this of our experience: "Intellectually, I have long known of the Seder, but now I know it experientially. To taste the horseradish with the honey is to know with our senses and therefore not to be forgotten that life holds for all of us both the bitter and the sweet."

The Quaker Family—Wednesday. It so happened that the Quaker family day came on the day of the peace vigil in Albany. For once the vigil was racially and culturally mixed.

The silent grace of the Quakers with the holding of hands around the table seemed to bring not only a feeling of closeness, but together, with the peace vigil in mind, we held also the people around the world, especially the victims of the Vietnam war.

The old-fashioned games (three-legged race; potato race; Quaker, Quaker, how art thou?) after the evening meal broke the seriousness of the vigil mood; but the mood was picked up again with the reading of the story of White Feather, followed by a spirited discussion of nonviolence. The story, as we know, is a true one of colonial days in New York State. The Indians, angered at the white man, were on the warpath, killing as they went. The Quakers remained in silent worship in their unlocked meeting house near Easton, New York. When the Indians came in they sensed in the silence the goodwill toward them, so they sat down and joined in the silent worship. On leaving, the chief put a white feather over the door; it was to signal all other Indians that here were truly friends of theirs.

In the ensuing discussion, samples were given of situations past and present when nonviolence had been successful. However, our more militant participants reminded us that, regardless of the Quakers' use of nonviolence toward the Indians, the white man kept on murdering them and stealing their land. "A whole nation of people was murdered. What do you expect us Negroes to do today, take it?"

The pacifist could only answer that when nonviolence is really tried, it works. But we went to bed that night with a renewed conviction that the task for us white liberals, as we have been told over and over, is truly to work on our own attitudes, and to see ourselves as others see us.

The Mountain Family—Thursday. Pearl Hall, a member of our mountain family read aloud during two meals the children's story of the *Fiddler on High Lonesome* by Brinton Turkle—fascinating, beautiful, and related to our feelings about relationships of people. We could hardly wait to hear what would happen next to this sensitive lad whose music made pacifists out of wild animals but failed to do so with his mountaineer family. The tragic symbolism bore down upon us. But life goes on, it seems, until we learn our lessons.

That evening, the mountaineers led us with a guitar in singing folksongs, dancing the Virginia reel, and sitting around a campfire. The songs we sang under the stars were those we all knew except a freedom song new to most of us:

> *Don't you know*
> *Time o' Time,*
> *Discord is in our land,*
> *People must take a stand.*

It seemed that our Harlem friends wanted to turn even our singing together into the urgency of today's crisis. What does this say to us comfortable middle-class whites?

The Harlem Family—Friday. The Harlem family said it in many ways—in the vocal grace before meals, in the chosen hymns and prayer at worship fellowship, in the "soul" food at dinner, and in the evening in the role-play of a day in a Harlem family. What did they say? "We want to be ourselves. Freedom now, with enough income and quality education to really be ourselves." This sense of urgency kept this particular group of American Negroes from paying attention to their so-called African heritage. Knowing that many Negroes are paying attention to this, we had borrowed from a friend who had just returned from Ghana some African things (some books, a drum, some strips of hand-woven cloth for women's dresses, masks and beads). But these things remained untouched on the mantel where they had been arranged.

The evening role-play of "A Day in the Life of a Harlem Family on Welfare" made a terrific impact on us middle-class liberal whites. Mrs. W., using her own children, role-played the difficulties of living in an unheated apartment, no private bath, and having to deal with the arrogant, two-faced white landlord, and the cold-hearted, know-it-all welfare worker. Running through the difficulties was the humor. We middle-class Americans know intellectually about all this, for we have read the sociological analyses like Kenneth Clark's *Black Ghetto*. But seeing it realistically acted out by those who must live with it is "something else again."

However, more was to come, and this spontaneously, when Mrs. W. was asked about how she and others had organized their neighbors and forced the city to build an overpass at 129th Street and Lexington Avenue in New York City, so that their children could safely cross the traffic-filled street to get to their play park. This was done, after all other kinds of pleading failed, by taking their own children, over a hundred of them, and sitting with them in the middle of the street, stopping the traffic. Even the act of being arrested and the treatment by the cops was role-played. Peals of laughter ran through the spontaneous dramatization. But the women won, and the overpass was built.

Our dance of the evening before going to bed was the Bugaloo! Even the Quakers had fun dancing it.

The Puerto Rican Family—Saturday. The beautiful Puerto Rican family and their "adopted relatives" had been eagerly waiting all week for their time to have a place in our sun of fellowship. At mealtime came the food—rice and beans, and chicken cooked as Puerto Ricans cook it. The games on the lawn in which the oldest and youngest could participate were most exciting and full of laughter. In the common room, we were introduced to the Puerto Rican type of a progressive party, which they call a *parranda*. One family visits another, babies and all. They sing and dance, share food, and then that family joins the ever-enlarging group. Our Powell House families got themselves in the different corners of the common room, and we all acted out the *parranda*. The singing and dancing flowed spontaneously out of the action. It all ended in one long, conga-like dance.

MORNING SESSIONS: Group Conversations and Discussions for Adults

In the mornings we used Group Conversation the first hour to bring out ways in which as children we had in our own families been made to feel important, ways which gave us a sense of closeness and of responsibility. This process also served quickly to bring this group into a deeper sense of fellowship. The second hour was a discussion bringing out various viewpoints about family life: today, what values and customs should be held on to, what changed? These were typical questions and comments:

> "Can we make our family life more democratic, such as in sharing the making of decisions more than we do?"
>
> "With young people today the new morality is that you can do anything you want as long as you don't hurt anybody."
>
> "The Judeo-Christian tradition must be observed—but that's hogwash to today's young people."
>
> "What would be the effect on family life of the guaranteed annual income for all people who need it? For one thing, it would bring the fathers back into the homes."
>
> "You whites are not trying to see that my children have the same kind of good education as yours. We get the worst teachers. How long must we take the crumbs from your table?"
>
> "Could we start a project for exchanging our children something like the Field Service does with high school children from another country?"

In the discussion one member quoted from Farson's *The Future of the Family:*

> It is the total family that will be changing, not the children. This will hold true in the realms of values, character formation, learning, and so on. And given the total family unit, there is now social technology available to help each family living its own future—gaming techniques, group process techniques, and so on. The family can become a learning unit that

can plan, discuss, debate and revise its own small society in ways never before possible.*

RECREATION: Arts and crafts (mainly for children) in the morning under the trees; swimming, volleyball, and nature walks kept adults and children creatively active. "Who wants to go fishing?" There were many answers of "I do." "Let's go dig for worms." So the children followed Bob Bacon as if he were the Pied Piper of Hamelin. "I caught a little fish but I put him back in the water," said a ten-year-old Harlem boy. His action was praised by one of the listening oldsters: "Then you gave him back his life."

Problems? Of course! The Quaker worship based on silence was uncomfortable for those not used to it, and rock 'n' roll music in the bedrooms hardly satisfied the Quakers, but when the Harlemites conducted worship service on their day and sang "Precious Lord, Take My Hand," we all felt close in the silence which followed.

Also, the teenagers gave us a shock. We adults had settled down to a midweek morning Group Conversation and discussion period when four teenagers entered the room with printed paper banners: "More action." "Less talk." "Stamp out group discussion." "We want volleyball." We sat dumbfounded. "Break it up," they commanded firmly. And we did.

It was a mind-expanding experience to feel the force of these teenagers. We all went out into the bright sunshine and played volleyball. But volleyball can't last forever. The adults started drifting to chairs under the trees. Suddenly real communication blossomed. Now that "Whitey" wasn't having all the ideas, the talk poured out. We were treated to jumbo-sized helpings of life in the ghettos, and it was obvious in what ways we could help. After that, the group discussion format was abandoned, and we adults came together spontaneously to talk over leadership techniques for better race relations and intercultural exchange in our back-home communities.

RESULTS: If it's feelings you want, we got over many emotional hurdles. Black *is* beautiful. If it's back-home follow-up, we all plan to work together in our neighborhoods, but only a few of us lived near enough. We are glad that plans for the next venture of

* Richard E. Farson, et al. (New York, Family Service Association). Of related interest: *Cojoint Family Therapy* by Virginia Satir.

this sort involve selecting families from nearby neighborhoods, so that during the year they can continue their fellowship and work on common problems.

As for results on individuals: One middleclass person spent the rest of the summer tutoring ghetto children rather than spending weekends in the country—as indicated in the statement introducing this section.

Several children have kept contact with their "pretend" families through birthday and Christmas cards. One ten-year-old, when talking with his mother months after the experience, said: "Don't you remember David? He's my Jewish uncle."

What of the Future?

What does this fascinating and valuable intercultural experience say to program planners in family life and in religious and secular education?

The changing relationships among our various ethnic groups have pointed up the pressing need to explore and experiment in homes, schools and community groups with possible next steps in intergroup relationships. Much attention is being paid to developing new relationships between black and white Americans, but serious also is the need to look at relationships with Indian Americans, Mexican Americans, Puerto Rican Americans, as well as the third-, fourth- and fifth-generation Americans of various cultural backgrounds. The National Education Association recently issued a statement as a reason for exploring next steps in intercultural education:

> America has paid great homage to the concept of the "melting pot," but the significant fact about the melting pot is that it didn't happen for all . . . The choice open to members of a disparate culture or community is to assimilate and disappear or to be isolated and relegated to second-class citizenship— or no citizenship at all as in the case of the first Americans.

We would suggest a third alternative to the disappearance of an ethnic group or second-class citizenship. It would be a massive attempt on the part of all our educational institutions—home, school and various community organizations, as well as the mass media—

to dramatize the customs (ways of doing things) of the many ethnic groups in our midst in ways which would be to "celebrate each other's existence" just because of our interesting cultural differences. Through this sharing and spontaneous cultural cross-fertilization of the best of each group, a richer American culture would surely evolve. This hunger to find himself explains a part of the frustration of the American black who for generations has not been allowed to be himself in American life.

If we could participate in the process of intercultural face-to-face experiences, we might be freed from our fear of living next door to or being in the same school and neighborhood with families whose customs differ from our own, not to mention the potential of being able to work more harmoniously on our common problems of living together. Then, too, the giving of community social recognition to the best of one's cultural backgrounds tends to make us want to live up to that best.

There is an old Quaker proverb which might help us Americans in our time of crisis: "It's the not-me in thee which makes thee valuable to me." The wisdom in this proverb is simple and profound—it's that differences are to be valued as integral with the sacredness of human personality. They can be of many sorts, e.g. age, sex, class, profession, religion, or ethnicity—for we can each grow from understanding, perhaps even imbibing something of the other's experience—and the values back of those experiences. While in this manual we may seem, because of the present civil-rights struggle, to focus mainly on the black experience in America, Group Conversation was started in the 1940s around the concern to relate our various ethnic and religious groups to each other in a positive way. Group Conversation was created as a way to help us accept each other by accepting ourselves—a way of seeing that our very differences can make our common American life richer and more interesting for all of us.

Today we Americans are on the move, our competitive system thrusts us upward. Can we carry with us any of our inherited cultural differentials? Citizens of our cities everywhere are being implored to build more functional neighborhoods—to meet together around common problems. Will these new neighborhoods be separated cultural islands, will they be made up of homes alike both inside and out? Will we be crushing out of existence our remaining ethnic differences, leaving only cultural sterility, or will we begin now consciously to try to make a creative use of differences? Can we not take the time to meet in small groups, sharing not just our grievances but our interesting family and ethnic customs as well as our aspirations, even our laughter and our tears?

It was in such a group that we first met Swift Eagle. Along with others in that New York City home gathering, he shared with us his customs, his Arizona experiences of festivities in the spring of the year. He told us of the corn dance and the prayer for rain, and then spontaneously he led us (a very mixed group) in a Buffalo Dance. With him, we felt at one with the wind, the rain, with animals, man and God. In the ensuing discussions we sometimes wondered if "a more creative use of leisure" should in our technological, time-freeing age be given priority equal to "the discipline of work." Who can lead the way as we move into our new neighborhoods, made up of all kinds of Americans, yet Americans all? Will it be the blacks, with their urgency and their spontaneity and creativity, or will it be all of us together? *

But there will be no new neighborhoods worth moving into unless we can rid ourselves of war, poverty and racism. We have been told this by our most brilliant, concerned and dedicated leaders— but none more concerned or dedicated than was Martin Luther King Jr. Nor did he confine his admonitions to us Americans. He knew and said on more than one occasion that these three great modern evils, as bad as they are here, are not confined to the United States: "If we do not rid ourselves of racism, militarism and economic exploitation, the curtain will go down on Western white civilization." Europeans all too easily see the American race problem as peculiarly ours and are blinded to the same attitude of prejudice in their countries toward the "strangers in their midst"— the millions of foreign workers from southern Europe who have migrated north to do the unskilled work so needed in the rebuilding of cities. And England has its Pakistanis and East and West Indians who are unwelcome. It is not enough to pass protective ordinances which give these strangers some security. People want and need more than security. They want a sense of belonging, of worthiness, even love. It is our belief that these ingredients are needed for

* The past generation of sociologists predicted the disappearance of ethnicity, but more recent studies, especially those headed by Patrick Moynihan and Andrew W. Greely, show an undreamed-of tenacity on the part of different levels in ethnic groups to hold on and stand apart.

releasing human potential in all peoples in all lands. We believe that these ingredients will not be added to the amalgam of community life in any country unless sensitive individuals work at it, preparing themselves seriously and persistently, as persistently as did the great souls of the past. For today this work of developing harmonious relationships must be done by millions of "little people," not only in day-to-day contacts but in small groups. We will demonstrate, because it is true, that life is one organic whole, and that not to give to and receive from people who have come from different parts of that whole is to live less than completely.

Annotated Bibliography

Methods of Working with Groups

Adult Education Association of the U.S.A., *How to Use Role Playing,* Leadership Pamphlet No. 6 (Washington, AEA, 1956).

DuBois, Rachel Davis, *Get Together Americans* (New York, Harper & Bros., 1943).

———, *Neighbors in Action* (New York, Harper & Bros., 1950). A detailed report of how the home and school working together under the PTA changed the atmosphere of a whole neighborhood by using the method of Group Conversation.

Lippitt, Gordon, *Improving Decision Making with Groups* (Washington, D.C., National Education Association).

Miles, Matthew, *Learning to Work in Groups* (New York, Columbia University Press, 1959). A book addressed to the practitioner in the school and in other institutions who seeks to improve his own work. An "attempt to bring together what is now known about the practical problem of helping people learn better group behavior."

Thelen, Herbert A., *Dynamics of Groups at Work* (Chicago, University of Chicago Press, 1954).

Gordon, Thomas, *Group-Centered Leadership,* (Boston, Houghton-Mifflin Co., 1955).

Understanding Ethnic Minorities

NEGRO AMERICANS

The following six books are all basic to an understanding of the Negro in American life.

Bontemps, Arna and Hughes, Langston, eds., *Book of Negro Folk-*

147

lore (New York, Dodd, Mead & Co., 1958). Stories, games, tales of animals, memories of slavery, spirituals.

FAUSET, ARTHUR HUFF, and BRIGHT, NELLIE RATHBONE, *America, Red, White, Black, Yellow* (Philadelphia, Franklin Publishing Co., 1969). A fascinating elementary grade history of the peoples of America, leaving out none of them. The numerous pictures and the division into study units make the book valuable to the teacher as well as to the pupil.

LOGAN, RAYFORD W., *The Negro in the United States* (New York, Van Nostrand-Reinhold, Anvil Books, 1957).

QUARLES, BENJAMIN, *The Negro in the Making of America* (New York, Macmillan, Collier Books, 1964).

ROSE, ARNOLD MARSHALL, *The Negro in America* (New York, Harper & Bros., 1948).

WOODSON, CARTER, *The Negro in Our History* (Washington, Associated Publishers, 1959).

MALCOLM X (with ALEX HALEY), *Autobiography of Malcolm X,* (New York, Grove, 1965). An impressive account, beginning with the childhood and youth, which in effect destined him for conversion to Black Muslimism. His later conversion to Islam, in the true sense of the word, and subsequent development of his thought, suggest he might have become a powerful figure in the Negro revolt.

BENNETT, LERONE, *Before the Mayflower: A History of the Negro in America—1619-1962* (Chicago, Johnson Pub. Co., 1963). A panoramic history of Negro life in America, dispelling some popular notions and accepted myths. It traces the history of Negro life from the Jamestown slaves to the "Second Reconstruction" of Martin Luther King, Jr., and today's Freedom Movement.

BILLINGSLEY, ANDREW, *Black Families in White America* (Englewood Cliffs, N.J., Prentice-Hall, 1968). The social and moral conditions of Negroes.

BONTEMPS, ARNA, ed., *American Negro Poetry* (New York, Hill and Wang, 1965). A representative anthology of poetry reflecting the Harlem Renaissance, including Langston Hughes, James Weldon Johnson and such contemporary poets as LeRoi Jones and Gwendolyn Brooks. The introduction by Arna Bontemps gives background material.

BOYD, MALCOLM, *As I Live and Breathe* (New York, Random House, 1969). Fragments of an autobiography.

BRANDT, JOSEPH R., *Why Black Power?* (New York, Friendship Press, 1968).

BROWN, CLAUDE, *Manchild in the Promised Land* (New York, Macmillan, 1965). The real hero of this hard-hitting autobiographical novel is the Harlem street where living boils out of the over-crowded slums and even the "fittest" must struggle to survive. The book offers an opportunity to get away from statistics and to learn about individual lives.

CLARKE, J. H., ed., *Malcolm X: The Man and His Time* (New York, Macmillan, 1969). A selection of books and articles relating to the life of Malcolm X, compiled by A. Peter Bailey.

CLEAVER, ELDRIDGE, *Soul on Ice* (New York, McGraw-Hill Book Co., and Delta Books, 1968). An eloquent black man speaks his mind on American society. A book at once stirring, disquieting, enlightening.

CONE, JAMES A., *Black Theology and Black Power* (New York, Seabury Press, 1969). Shows the growing willingness of black Christians to accept the difference imputed to them and to glorify it.

CULLEN, COUNTEE, *Caroling Dusk* (New York, Harper & Bros., 1927).

FRANKLIN, JOHN HOPE and STARR, ISIDORE, eds. *The Negro in the 20th Century* (New York, Random House, Vintage Books, 1969). A reader on the struggle for civil rights.

FRANKLIN, JOHN HOPE, ed., *Three Negro Classics* [WASHINGTON, BOOKER T., *Up from Slavery;* DU BOIS, W.E.B., *The Souls of Black Folk;* JOHNSON, JAMES W., *Autobiography of an Ex-colored Man*] (New York, Avon Books, 1965). The reading of these classics is basic to an understanding of historic and social background of our American race problem.

GREGORY, DICK, *From the Back of the Bus* (New York, E. P. Dutton & Co., and Avon Books, 1962). A good use of humor in releasing tensions.

———, *Nigger* (New York, Dutton, 1964). Dick Gregory's autobiography is written with the freshness of spirit and emphasis on service and aspiration that we would naturally expect from a man whose humor is cogent and whose life is well spent.

GRIER, WM. H., and COBBS, PRICE M., *Black Rage* (New York, Basic Books, 1968). Negroes and psychology.

HENTOFF, NAT, ed., *Black Anti-Semitism and Jewish Racism* (New York, Baron, 1970). Collected essays by four black and six Jewish authors. Points out the need for blacks to run their own businesses, compares their rise to similar cases of Irish, Jewish businesses in the slums. Talks of the blacks' need to "elevate and empower" themselves.

HUGHES, LANGSTON, *Famous Negro Heroes of America* (New York, Dodd, 1958). For grades 7-9, includes biographies of Ralph Bunche, Marian Anderson and others.

———, *The First Book of Jazz* (New York, Franklin Watts, 1955). In this book Langston Hughes relates how the exciting rhythms of jazz evolved from experiences of the people; from African drums, the cotton plantations, spirituals, blues and the city's brass bands.

———, *Five Plays* (Bloomington, Indiana University Press, 1963). "Mulatto," "Little Ham" & others.

———, *I Wonder as I Wander: An Autobiographical Journey* (New York, Hill & Wang, 1964).

———, *Selected Poems* (New York, Knopf, 1959).

HILL, HERBERT, ed., *Anger and Beyond—The Negro Writer in the United States* (New York, Harper & Row, 1966). Essays by ten

Negro and white writers on American Negro literature. One of the best.

HOUGH, JOSEPH C., *Black Power and White Protestants* (New York, Oxford University Press, 1968).

JOHNSON, JAMES W., *Book of American Negro Poetry* (New York, Harcourt, Brace & World, 1931).

———, *God's Trombones* (New York, Viking Press, 1927). The dramatic sermons of Southern Negro preachers put in poetic form. A classic.

LINCOLN, C. ERIC, *Is Anybody Listening to Black America?* (New York, Seabury, 1968).

———, *Sounds of the Struggle* (New York, Wm. Morrow and Co., 1968).

LECKY, ROBERT S. and WRIGHT, H. ELLIOT, eds., *Black Manifesto: Religion, Racism and Reparation* (New York, Sheed & Ward, 1970). An explanation of the black turn toward the Church both for money as well as social and moral leadership in the struggle for improvement.

MEIER, AUGUST and RUDWICK, ELLIOTT, eds., *Making of Black America, The* (New York, Atheneum, 1969). The origins of black Americans and the black community in America.

National Advisory Commission on Civil Disorders. *Report of the National Advisory Commission on Civil Disorders* [Otto Kerner, chairman]; foreword by Tom Wicker (New York, E. P. Dutton, 1968). The authoritative picture of our nation divided by race. Should be read by all committed workers on the problem.

RUSTIN, BAYARD, "The Failure of Black Separatism" (New York, *Harper's*, Vol. 240, Jan. 1970, pp. 25-34). Descriptions of economic alternatives to boost the black's income and discussion of how various attempts at black separated industries have failed to date. The whole question of where improved opportunities for jobs and money for blacks will come from is explored.

SACHS, WULF, *Black Anger* (New York, Grove Press, 1969).

SCHEER, ROBERT, ed., *Eldridge Cleaver* (New York, Random House, 1969). Post-prison writings and speeches, with an appraisal by the editor.

THURMAN, HOWARD, *The Luminous Darkness* (New York, Harper & Row, 1965). A personal interpretation of the anatomy of segregation and the ground of hope.

Urban America, Inc. and The Urban Coalition, *One Year Later* (New York, Praeger, 1969). An assessment of the nation's response to the crisis described by the National Advisory Commission on Civil Disorders.

WALKER, MARGARET, *For My People* (New Haven, Yale University Press, 1943). A poetic tribute to the American Negro.

WARREN, ROBERT PENN, *Who Speaks for the Negro?* (New York, Random House, 1965). Interviews with Negro leaders.

WASHINGTON, JOSEPH R., JR., *The Politics of God* (Boston, Beacon

Press, 1967). Church and race relations; the Negro and his religion.

YOUNG, WHITNEY M., JR., *Beyond Racism: Building an Open Society* (New York, McGraw-Hill, 1970). What the black race wants, what are its needs in its search for the "new land."

CHILDREN IN THE GHETTO

BIBBY, CYRIL, *Race Prejudice and Education* (New York, Praeger, 1960). This book is an outcome of the Seventh Session of the General Conference of UNESCO. For the teacher who wishes to deal honestly with race and race relations.

CLARK, KENNETH B., *Dark Ghetto: Dilemmas of Social Power;* foreword by Gunnar Myrdal (New York, Harper, 1965). Taking his point of departure from the HARYOU report, *Youth in the Ghetto,* the author here goes on to examine the ugly facts of the ghetto everywhere and for all its denizens, and to articulate the minimum requirements for a genuine obliteration of ghetto barriers.

COLES, ROBERT, *Children of Crisis—A Study of Courage and Fear* (Boston, Little, Brown, 1964). A study by a psychiatrist of the impact of desegregation on the people of the South, black and white, young and old. A stark portrayal of the chronic violence which has permeated race relations. A moving document of the struggle of persons caught up in dramatic social change.

DUNCAN, ETHEL M., *Democracy's Children* (New York, Hinds, Hayden & Eldredge, 1945). A fifth-grade teacher reports on classroom and assembly seasonal and inter-group programs worked out with her pupils.

GLASSER, W., *Schools Without Failure* (New York, Harper & Row, 1969).

HENTOFF, NAT, *Our Children Are Dying* (New York, Viking, 1966). Description of the problems faced by a ghetto school in New York (P.S. 119), and its remarkable principal, Elliot Schapiro.

HOLT, JOHN, *How Children Fail* (New York, Pitman, 1964). Based on the perceptive and disconcerting observations of an unusual classroom teacher, it describes the ways in which teacher and pupil strategies in school combine to prevent real learning from taking place.

————, *How Children Learn* (New York, Pitman, 1967). A book as sensitive as his first one. It describes how children learn spontaneously before they have been made afraid to venture and explore, and before they have developed strategies for producing the simulation of achievement—parroting of answers instead of thinking—which is so often demanded by adults, parents and teachers alike.

JERSILD, ARTHUR, *When Teachers Face Themselves* (New York, Teachers College, Columbia, 1955). A discussion of teachers' feelings, especially feelings of anxiety, loneliness, hostility, compassion, and the search for meaning.

KOZOL, JONATHAN, *Death at an Early Age* (New York, Bantam Books, 1967). How a school system destroys children's growth.

RIESSMAN, FRANK, *The Culturally Deprived Child* (New York, Harper & Row, 1962). This perceptive author notes some overlooked positive qualities in children considered "deprived." Valuable to help some parents overcome fear of integrated schools.

TRUBOWITZ, SIDNEY, *A Handbook for Teaching in the Ghetto School* (Chicago, Quadrangle Books, 1968). A practical yet compassionate book by a Manhattan school principal—"Ghetto schools need our best teachers." This book helps the teacher to communicate with the ghetto child.

BOOKS BY AND ABOUT MARTIN LUTHER KING, JR.

BENNETT, LERONE, JR., *What Manner of Man* (Chicago, Johnson Pub. Co., 1964). This biography of Martin Luther King, Jr. shows the step-by-step growth into the great leader which he became. It contains his *Dream* speech. Especially valuable for young people.

KING, CORETTA SCOTT, *My Life with Martin Luther King, Jr.* (New York, Holt, Rinehart and Winston, 1969). An affectionate portrayal of the man in the throes of his work and in his relationships with his family and fellow workers.

KING, MARTIN LUTHER, JR., *Why We Can't Wait* (New York, Harper, 1964 and Signet Books). This work is among the most vigorous statements of Dr. King's philosophy on nonviolence. He stresses the important gains by Negroes in its use.

————, *Where Do We Go from Here: Chaos or Community?* (New York, Harper & Row, 1967). In this book Dr. King is eloquent about "What is Black Power?" "It is the strength required to bring about social, political or economic changes. In this sense power is not only desirable but necessary in order to implement the demands of love and justice."

JEWISH AMERICANS

BELFORD, LEE A., *Introduction to Judaism* (New York, Association Press, 1961). An explanation of some of the beliefs and practices of Jews through the world.

BERNARD, ROSE, *Hebraic Festivals; A Haggadah of Our Time; Hanukah, The Festival of Lights; Songs around the Table Z'mirot.* A series of four pamphlets simplified for participation and use by Jews and non-Jews.

EISENSTEIN, IRA, *Judaism under Freedom* (New York, Jewish Reconstructionist Press, 1956). Approaches to the problems of adjustment in the democratic society in the U.S. and Israel.

EPSTEIN, BENJAMIN, and FORSTER, ARNOLD, *Some of My Best Friends,* (New York, Farrar, Straus, 1962).

FREEHOF, S.B., *Reform Jewish Practice* (New York, Block Pub. Co., 1963).

GASTER, THEODORE, *Festivals of the Jewish Year* (New York, Sloane, 1953). A modern interpretation and guide to fasts and feasts.

KAPLAN, MORDECAI, *Judaism as a Civilization* (New York, Schocken Books, 1967). Fundamental ethical and spiritual concepts in Judaism reinterpreted. Toward a reconstruction of American Jewish Life.

KERTZER, MORRIS, *What Is a Jew* (Cleveland, World Pub. Co., 1960). Questions most commonly asked.

RACHIN, MOSES, *Promised Land: New York's Jews, 1870-1914* (New York, Harcourt, 1962). How New York City became the haven for the oppressed Jew.

SCHAUSS, HAYYIM, *The Jewish Festivals* (Cincinnati, University of American Hebrew Congregations, 1938).

SCHOENER, A., *Portal to America: The Lower East Side: 1870-1925.* (New York, Holt, Rinehart & Winston, 1967). How the Lower East Side became the gateway to mobility for the American Jew.

AMERICAN INDIANS

The American Heritage Book of Indians, (New York, American Heritage, Simon and Schuster, 1969).

BROWN, FRANCIS J., and ROUCEK, JOSEPH, eds., *One America: Our Racial and National Minorities* (New York, Prentice-Hall, 1945).

BROWN, JOSEPH EPES, *The Spiritual Legacy of the American Indian* (Wallingford, Pa., Pendle Hill Pamphlets, 1964). Reverence for nature and for life is central to his religion. The beautiful creation myths of the Plains Indians are amazingly similar to the biblical Genesis.

CAHN, EDGAR, *Our Brother's Keeper* (Washington, Citizen's Advocate).

COLLIER, JOHN, *Indians of the Americas* (New York, Mentor Books, New American Library, 1959). The author invites us to consider the way of the American Indians, for he sees in their way of life the hope and the fate of mankind.

DELORIA, VINE, *Custer Died for Your Sins* (New York, Macmillan, 1969). This Indian leader writes a critical and jarring criticism of the past role of the Christian missionary in the life of the Indian. He uses humor but not bitterness.

FUCHS, ESTELLE, "Time to Redeem an Old Promise" (*Saturday Review*, Jan. 24, 1970, pp. 54 ff.). The problems of schooling American Indian children in terms of differences of cultural and educational goals are analyzed. Emphasis is placed on Indian heritage, the need for teaching English as a second language, and on the development of a realistic course to prepare children for vocations and careers.

GLAZER, NATHAN and MOYNIHAN, DANIEL PATRICK, *Beyond the Melting Pot* (Cambridge, M.I.T. Press, 1963). The Negroes, Puerto Ricans, Jews, Italians, and Irish of New York City.

GREELEY, ANDREW M., *Why Can't They Be Like Us?* (New York, Institute of Human Relations Press, 1969). Facts and fallacies about ethnic differences and group conflicts in America.

JOSEPHY, ALVIN, *The Indian Heritage in America,* (New York, Knopf, 1969). The author has lived with Indians for some 20 years and writes of their history up to the present.

STEINER, STAN, *The New Indians* (New York, Harper & Row, 1968). The author, trusted by the Indian, details the modern Indians' "uprising—ideological, social, legal, political. Red power is his cry, a full-scale report."

ITALIAN, MEXICAN AND PUERTO RICAN AMERICANS

EVANS, JEAN, *Three Men* (New York, Grove, 1950). The first of the "Three Men," Johnny Rocco, is Italian, the son of a poor family living in a slum. His life also, like that of Claude Brown and Piri Thomas, exemplifies the "Culture of Poverty."

LEWIS, OSCAR, *La Vida—A Puerto Rican Family in the Culture of Poverty: San Juan and New York.* (New York, Random House, 1966).

STEINER, STAN, *La Raza—The Mexican American* (New York, Harper & Row, 1970). The author examines the past, present and future of "chicanos" in the southwestern United States. He suggests a cultural readiness and political sophistication of which "Anglos" are wholly unaware.

THOMAS, PIRI, *Down These Mean Streets* (New York, Signet, 1967). A first-person account of the Puerto Rican experience in New York City.

ORIENTAL AMERICANS

GLICK, CARL, *Shake Hands with the Dragon* (New York, McGraw-Hill Book Co., 1941).

————, *Three Times I Bow* (New York, Whittlesey House, 1943).

SUNG, B. L., *Mountain of Gold* (New York, Macmillan, 1967). An account of the Chinese in America during the gold rush to today.

Understanding the Nature of Prejudice

ADORNO, T. W., and Others, *The Authoritarian Personality* (New York, Harper & Bros., 1950). A study of the personality traits of people who are especially susceptible to antidemocratic propaganda. It suggests that those who show the greatest susceptibility to fascist propaganda have many traits in common.

ALLPORT, GORDON W., *The Nature of Prejudice* (New York, Doubleday Anchor Books, 1958). A comprehensive and penetrating study of the origin and nature of prejudice.

BOYLE, SARAH PATTON, *The Desegregated Heart* (New York, William Morrow, Apollo Editions, 1962). The author, a Virginian of good family and liberal mind, tells of her experiences as she sets out to improve race relations in her home town. This book is a deeply felt study of the self-examination she undertakes when she is rebuffed by those she tries to help and disillusioned by those upon whose help she had depended.

Crisis in America: Hope through Action (New York, Friendship Press, 1968). An outline for an action study task force in the field of race relations.

CLARK, KENNETH B., *Prejudice and Your Child* (Boston, Beacon Press, 1965). This authoritative work shows the effects on Negro and white children of societal pressures toward racial awareness. It illuminates the fundamental moral conflict in the white and the feeling of inferiority in the Negro child.

HIRSH, SELMA, *The Fears Men Live By* (New York, Harper & Bros., 1955). A discussion of the positive methods that can be applied to reducing the fears and dispelling the stereotyped images that distort our values.

UNESCO, *The Race Question in Modern Science: Race and Science* (New York, Columbia University Press, 1961). A summary of the thinking of social and behavioral scientists from many nations about the nature and problem of race.

VAN DER POST, LAURENS, *The Dark Eye in Africa* (New York, William Morrow, 1955). Of the many white people writing about Africa, van der Post is, no doubt, one of the most sensitive to the feelings of the Africans. His central thesis is that Europeans reject the natural in themselves. This becomes projected on the Negro and turns into fear and hatred. One chapter gives his views on this attitude as applied to the American race problem.

A PHILOSOPHY OF CULTURAL DIVERSITY

BIGELOW, KARL W., Co-ordinator, *Lectures at Conference on Education Problems of Special Cultural Groups* (New York, Bureau of Publications, Teachers College, Columbia University, 1951). Cultural diversity is here presented on a world basis by lecturers from several countries.

DUBOIS, RACHEL DAVIS, *Build Together Americans* (New York: Hinds, Hayden & Eldredge, 1945). In a report of a project in several schools, by appreciating and sharing cultural values of our ethnic groups a creative use of differences was evolved in the intercultural education project by several secondary schools reported here. A valuable bibliography of basic books in the field.

———, *Neighbors in Action* (New York, Harper & Bros., 1950). The sharing and creative use of cultural differences in this report was evolved in this intercultural education project on the elementary school level. Special attention was given to the integration of the Puerto Rican with other cultural groups.

SPICER, DOROTHY GLADYS, *Folk Festivals and the Foreign Community,* (New York, Woman Press, 1923).

Understanding the Problem of Poverty

ABRAMS, CHARLES, *Forbidden Neighbors* (New York, Harper & Bros., 1955). A study of prejudice in housing in the United States, with a suggested program for individual and governmental action.

ELMAN, RICHARD, *Poorhouse State—The American Way of Life on Public Assistance* (New York, Random House, 1966). The welfare system in action as seen through the eyes of the welfare recipient.

HARRINGTON, MICHAEL, *The Other America—Poverty in the United States* (New York, Macmillan, 1962). This book is a basic and important one even for those who may be thought of as well informed. Because of the disproportionately large number of Negroes who belong to the impoverished class, Negro poverty is considered throughout Chapter 4. "If You're Black, Stay Back" is specifically concerned with the Negro.

HENTOFF, NAT, *New Equality* (New York, Viking, 1965). Firm, factual, sober of tone and objectively detached in manner, the author's program calls for a revolutionary reordering of society in the areas of unemployment, education and housing.

MOYNIHAN, DANIEL PATRICK, *On Understanding Poverty* (New York, Basic Books, Inc., 1969). Perspectives from the social sciences.

———, *Maximum Feasible Misunderstanding: Community Action in the War of Poverty* (Glencoe, Free Press, 1964).

RUSTIN, BAYARD, *A "Freedom Budget" for All Americans* (New York, A. Philip Randolph Institute, 1967). Pamphlet.

Human Potential and Alienation

ERIKSON, ERIK, *Identity—Youth and Crisis* (New York, Norton, 1968). The struggle for identity in the midst of contemporary problems.

FROMM, ERICH, *The Revolution of Hope—Toward a Humanized Technology* (New York, Bantam Books, 1968). An analysis of the alienation forces in contemporary society, and of measures which may counteract alienation.

JUNG, C. G., *The Undiscovered Self* (New York, Mentor Books, New American Library, 1958). Jung relies on the individual, on his need and capacity to know himself, as the only effective means of combating man's growing submergence in the mass, whether this be exemplified by submission to the collective state, adherence to religious needs, or the leveling process of scientific, statistical averages. Brief and readable.

———, *Modern Man in Search of a Soul.* (New York, Harcourt, 1939).

KENISTON, KENNETH, *The Uncommitted—Alienated Youth in American Society* (New York, Harcourt, Brace & World, 1965).

MASLOW, ABRAHAM H., *Toward a Psychology of Being* (Princeton, D. Van Nostrand Co., 1962). This modern psychologist puts into nonreligious terms some basic propositions relating among other things to "the contemplation and enjoyment of the innate life not only as a kind of 'action in itself' but because it produces stillness . . . and the ability to wait."

MEAD, MARGARET, *Culture and Commitment* (New York, Doubleday: Natural History Press, 1970). A study of the generation gap.

MURPHY, GARDNER, *Human Potentialities* (New York, Basic Books, Inc., 1958). One of America's foremost psychologists dramatically shows us how we can, by our free choices, control not only our own destinies, but those of the countless generations to come.

OVERSTREET, HARRY, *The Mature Mind* and *Mind Alive* (New York, Norton, 1949 and 1954). This author's books, putting modern psychological concepts into easy reading form, are excellent for starting a person's thinking along these lines.

PROGOFF, IRA, *The Symbolic and the Real* (New York, Julian Press, 1963). A new psychological approach to the fuller experience of personal existence.

ROGERS, CARL, *On Becoming a Person* (Boston, Houghton Mifflin, 1961). What is the meaning of personal growth? Under what conditions is such growth possible?

————, *Freedom to Learn* (Columbus, Charles Merrill, 1969). An invaluable book for the teacher concerned with meaningful learning. Rogers' position is that children and students can be trusted to learn when a facilitating person creates a climate in which the learner becomes responsibly involved in setting his own goals and implementing them.

TILLICH, PAUL, *The Courage to Be* (New Haven, Yale University Press, 1952).

TORRANCE, E. PAUL, *Guiding Creative Talent* (Englewood Cliffs, Prentice-Hall, 1962). What the schools can do to foster divergent thinking and creativity.

Spiritual Resources

BRINTON, HOWARD, *Friends for 300 Years* (New York, Harper & Bros., 1952). The history and beliefs of the Society of Friends since George Fox started the Quaker movement. "One of the great Quaker books of all time."

BUBER, MARTIN, *I and Thou*, 2nd. ed. (New York, Scribner, 1958). A basic book on Buber's philosophy.

CHASE, STUART, *Roads to Agreement* (New York, Harper & Bros.). The Quaker method of reaching consensus is compared with the voting process.

DE CHARDIN, PIERRE TEILHARD, *The Phenomenon of Man* (New York,

Harper & Row, 1959). "A great man of science and a great soul. His work gives our generation the comprehensive view it sorely needs."

————, *Hymn of the Universe* (New York, Harper & Row, 1961). The mystical quality of the world-famed scientist and priest is present here in the form of prose poems.

FRIEDMAN, MAURICE S., *Martin Buber: The Life of Dialogue* (New York, Harper Torchbooks, 1960). Dr. Friedman gives an interesting interpretation of the philosophy of Martin Buber, the Hebrew scholar and religious leader.

HOWE, REUEL L., *The Miracle of Dialogue* (New York, Seabury Press, 1963). In the broadest sense, Dr. Howe's book goes to the heart of the problems involved in creative communication and mature human relationships.

KELLY, THOMAS R., *A Testament of Devotion* (New York, Harper & Row, 1941). A Quaker classic. Especially valuable for dialogue purposes are the chapters on "The Blessed Community" and "The Simplification of Life."

KRUTCH, JOSEPH WOOD, *The Measure of Man* (New York, Grosset's Universal Library, 1954). In Chapter Seven and Nine the author shows that modern science now recognizes the mysterious.

SYKES, JOHN, *The Quakers* (Philadelphia, J. B. Lippincott, 1959). This study of the Friends, their history and their place in the modern world explains what Quakers basically stand for and why that stand is important. His descriptions of the meeting for worship and the meeting for business are excellent.

VINING, ELIZABETH GRAY, *The World in Tune* (New York, Harper, 1954). Thoughts on "minor ecstasies"—charmingly written.

Pamphlets

American Friends Service Committee. *Race and Conscience in America* (Norman, Okla., University of Oklahoma Press, 1959). Prepared by a working party of fourteen, this study of the impact of segregation on every American proclaims the authors' deep belief in the relevance of religious conviction and moral standards to these issues.

————, *Days of Discovery* (Philadelphia, American Friends Service Committee, 1960). A series of short pamphlets on seasons and holidays with suggestions for teachers and leaders.

Magazines

The Churchman (monthly), Protestant Episcopal. Churchman Publications, 1074 23rd Ave. N., St. Petersburg, Fla. 33704.

Ebony (monthly), Negro news and pictures. Johnson Publishing Co., 1820 S. Michigan Ave., Chicago, Ill. 60616.

Fellowship (monthly). Fellowship of Reconciliation, P.O. Box 271, Nyack, N.Y. 10960. Basically Christian but relates to all religious

groups and devoted to the use of nonviolent methods to change unjust conditions in our society.

Freedomways: A Quarterly Review of the Negro Freedom Movement.
Freedomways Association, Inc., 799 Broadway, New York, N. Y.
10003.

Negro Digest (monthly). Johnson Publishing Co., 1820 S. Michigan
Ave., Chicago, Ill. 60616. A serious magazine, in digest format, national in scope, with international distribution. Informative and well-
written.

New South: A Quarterly Review of Southern Affairs. Southern Regional Council, 5 Forsyth St., N.W., Atlanta, Ga. 30303. Although
this quarterly is scholarly and serious in intent, it remains close to
grass roots, is up to date and absorbing to read.

Tempo. A twice-monthly newsletter from the National Council of
Churches to "keep pace with the changing church." 475 Riverside
Drive, New York, N. Y. 10027.

DATE DUE

MAR 7 '72	MAY 16 '72		
NOV 13 '72	NOV 13 '72		
MAR 11 '74			
	APR 22 '74		
	OCT 27 '79		
OCT 31 '79			
NOV 19 '79	NOV 12 '79		